Someone to Watch Over Me

Living the Last Verse

Denny Kleibscheidel

xulon
PRESS

Copyright © 2006 by Denny Kleibscheidel

Someone to Watch Over Me
by Denny Kleibscheidel

Printed in the United States of America

ISBN 1-60034-218-3

All rights reserved solely by the author. The author guarantees all contents are original and do not infringe upon the legal rights of any other person or work. No part of this book may be reproduced in any form without the permission of the author. The views expressed in this book are not necessarily those of the publisher.

Unless otherwise indicated, Scripture quotations are taken from the HOLY BIBLE, NEW INTERNATIONAL VERSION®. NIV®. Copyright © 1973, 1978, 1984 by International Bible Society. Used by permission of Zondervan. All rights reserved.

Because He Lives used by permission. Words by William J. and Gloria Gaither. Music by William J. Gaither. Copyright © 1971 by William J. Gaither, Inc.

www.xulonpress.com

This book is dedicated to my wonderful son, Joseph Paul. My love for you inspired me to write this book. I pray its words will always be an inspiration to you.

"I love you my son, I'll always love you."

Dad

Contents

	Introduction	ix
1	Just Because He Lives	11
2	Boy Meets Girl	23
3	Just Friends	33
4	The Star Doesn't Shine	39
5	Invite that Boy to Church	45
6	No Surrender	51
7	Just As I Am	57
8	From This Day On	65
9	Rocky Mountain High	71
10	Worth the Wait	77
11	Breaking News	85
12	When I Am Weak I Am Strong	91
13	Time to Witness	101
14	Niagara Falls	109
15	Fear is Not an Option	119
16	Get Yourself Together	127
17	Do I Really Need a Turn?	133
18	Speaking Out	141
19	The Truth Hurts	147
20	No Sacrifice Is Too Big	157
21	Straight from the Heart	165
22	Joey's Greatest Gift	173
23	Broken Again	181
24	Time to Go Home	189
	Epilogue	191
	Contact	201

Introduction

*I*n 1980, I married Tracey, a young Christian full of life and lots of energy. Our early days together were not so different from other young couples. We had a traditional wedding and began our lives together filled with the same hopes and dreams of most ordinary people.

We combined our love for Jesus and our background in music to start a ministry to both the church and the lost. We were a typical Christian couple, strolling down life's highway void of any pitfalls or forks in the road.

Several years into our marriage, we had a son we named Joseph Paul. As our family was starting to grow, other changes began to occur; forcing us to realize that life would be far from typical.

With few warning signs, our journey detoured onto a much darker and rockier road. Tracey was diagnosed with bone cancer, resulting in the amputation of her left leg. It seemed as though life, as we knew it, had come to a screeching halt.

The following days and years saw their share of pain, disappointment, and loss. What might have resulted into a life of sadness and despair was transformed into a story of grace, hope, and witness.

Tracey lived for seven years after her diagnosis of cancer. Although our marriage was just a brief moment in time, God blessed that time with experiences measured only by *heavenly standards*.

As her husband and caregiver, I felt compelled to share our story of how God gave two ordinary people the opportunity to live extraordinary lives.

Chapter 1

Just Because He Lives

Friends and family filled the waiting area as the doctor performed a biopsy of the tumor in Tracey's leg. Everyone's emotions seemed to cloud our ability to comprehend what was happening, and why.

I was mostly concerned for Tracey's mom, Shirley. Consumed by worry, she looked as though she might collapse at any time. She was waiting for the hard news no mother should ever have to hear. The breaking of Shirley's heart for her precious daughter seemed to rival the pain of Tracey's broken leg.

The coldness of reality set in, making it hard for any of us to think positive thoughts. Instead, it seemed God was preparing us for whatever the report might be; even the worst.

I previously asked Dr. Leeson to talk with me confidentially. I told him I would explain everything to the others afterwards. You might call it a control thing but I didn't need any distractions while considering our future. My first obligation was to Tracey and the care she needed. I could help comfort others after I knew she received proper care.

When Dr. Leeson emerged, we went out into the hall where we could speak privately. I could tell by the look on his face there wasn't going to be any rejoicing that day. He explained that the tumor looked cancerous but we wouldn't know for sure until the results came back from the lab. I asked him to give me his gut feeling, to shoot straight from the hip for I was prepared.

He was almost positive we were dealing with cancer and would give us some options to consider later. He was quite apologetic to share such bad news. I assured him God was in control.

The next day Tracey and I waited for the doctor to come with the results. We were anxious to speak to him, yet cautious at the same time. We prayed together more than ever before, it always helped us to make good and clear decisions. We asked God to give wisdom to all the doctors so we could lean on them for guidance. Seeking God with all our heart not only drew us closer to him but also to each other. I knew Tracey was going to need me more than ever before. I just hoped to be worthy of the task.

When Dr. Leeson first entered the room, he asked how Tracey felt and if she was receiving good care. He wanted to make sure Tracey was getting enough medicine to keep her out of pain. Tracey was different from most, only accepting drugs whenever the pain was unbearable. She wanted to stay as alert as possible and would rather hurt than be out of it.

After assuring the doctor she was well cared for Tracey said, "You don't have to bother with a long speech. I already know what you're going to tell me. I know I have *cancer* and I've already accepted it. I'm ready to take the next step."

Even then, Tracey was thinking about the doctor's feelings more than worrying about herself. I watched her do this countless times, but was still amazed at how selfless she could be.

The doctor confirmed that it was definitely cancer then offered a couple of options for us to consider.

The *first option* was to take the most radical approach, which would be to amputate the leg to the hip. This choice would give the best opportunity to remove as much of the cancer as possible. Then, aggressive regiments of chemotherapy would follow the operation. He went on to explain what the prosthesis would look like if we opted for the decision to amputate. With much practice, Tracey would be able to walk adequately with it; just not enter any 100-yard dashes.

The *second option* was to save the leg by the combination of corrective surgery and chemotherapy. Tracey would need to stay in traction for six weeks while she underwent the chemo treatments. Afterwards, the doctor would then surgically remove the diseased femur bone along with enough muscle and tissue to establish good margins. A prosthetic device would then be implanted to take the place of the bone.

Tracey would still have her leg, but be left quite handicapped because of how much needed removed. I'm sure it was more complicated than that but it was enough for us to understand.

Tracey asked the doctor if he thought there was a good chance of her living a long life if we saved the leg. He explained that with this kind of cancer there was no guarantee even if we chose amputation. However, he was willing to try to save the leg if it was what Tracey wanted. Tracey had many more questions for the doctor so they continued talking for a while longer.

In the meantime, I just listened intently to everything Dr. Leeson had to say. When they were through with their discussion, I looked the doctor straight in the eye and said, "That's not a guinea pig lying in that bed. Let's say this is *your* wife. Now tell me what you would do."

He thought seriously about my question and answered frankly, "I'd amputate her leg. If it gave me just a fraction of a chance more of saving her life, I'd amputate."

"Then let's do it!" Tracey interrupted. "Let's cut it off!"

The doctor was taken back by Tracey's quick response. He said, "There's time for you to think about it, no decision needs to be made right away, you can take a few days if you want."

Tracey's reply was, "I don't need to think about it. I want to live and watch my little boy grow up. If having my leg removed can give me a greater chance to do that then that's what I want. I would rather live with one leg than die with two. Let's do it tomorrow."

As a Christian, Tracey already experienced a kind of "spiritual amputation." She realized as a teenager that sin was going to cause her to die. She underwent a "spiritual operation" when she accepted Jesus as her savior. He removed the "cancerous sin" and nailed it to a cross.

If this cancer was going to take Tracey's life then it was an easy decision to have it removed. There would be much pain and many scars to live with, but she would live. Living with cancer or sin is much more painful than having it removed. Not removing the cancer would cause Tracey to die in this present life; not removing her sin would cause her to die for eternity.

When Tracey was young, she and her friend Vicki went to a movie where one of the characters was a paraplegic. After the movie, Tracey shared with Vicki she believed God just revealed to her that she would be paralyzed or handicapped one day. Her friend found her statement a little morbid but thought nothing more of it. Some might say it was coincidental while others might just believe God was preparing Tracey for this day well in advance.

The doctor could not have performed the operation the next day even if he wanted. He had to check his calendar and schedule it with the hospital. Tracey told him she wanted to do it as soon as possible, it made no sense to her to let the cancer grow even one more day. Impressed by Tracey's spirit and courage, Dr. Leeson assured her he would make it happen.

After the doctor left, we cried and talked, then cried some more. Tracey looked into my eyes and asked, "Denny, will you still love me even if I only have one leg?"

Tracey needed to know that I would still want her and find her beautiful. She already knew the answers to those questions however hearing me say, "Yes, I'll still love you" gave her the added assurance she needed to help prepare for the operation.

Tracey guarded her feelings closely, only allowing herself to be vulnerable with me. It was okay even for the strongest person to feel those things. She knew no one understood her more than I did. I would never question her faith or think of her as being weak. I made sure she had no reason to doubt my devotion.

She started to sob saying, "I'm so sorry this is happening to us. I don't want to have to depend on anyone for anything. Poor little Joey is going to have to grow up with a handicapped mommy. I'll never be able to run with him or get down on the floor and play like other mommies. You'll have to do everything for him. Do you think he'll be embarrassed of me? What if I die and can't raise him?"

My heart broke more and more with every word. She continued to cry out to the point of making herself sick. The reality of cancer and the possibility of death were hitting her very hard.

I have never felt so sorry for anyone. I knew I needed to respond, but I felt so inadequate not knowing what to say. Realizing she had to purge herself of all those questions and fears, I told her to let it all out, and then waited for her to exhaust herself. Tracey cried until she could cry no more, using a whole box of tissues in the process.

We both sat in silence for a short while. I was afraid to say the wrong thing so I just stroked her face and hair. In classic Tracey fashion, she began to laugh saying, "Well wasn't that just stupid? Sorry, I just needed to vent a little." We both began to laugh until we cried, only this time with different tears.

I told her, "Remember the words from the wedding song I wrote for you, *"I'll be your strength if you weaken."* Well, now it's time for me to live out those words. I assure you that nothing, not even cancer, will destroy what we've worked so hard to build. I am certain God will protect Joey from everything that is happening. If you stand faithful, even on one leg, God will never leave us or forsake us.

"I promise I will never make you feel like a handicap. I'll consider it only a privilege to care for you, never a burden. I vow to do only what you ask me to do, allowing you to be as independent as you want to be."

Her eyes welled up with tears as she whispered, "That's why I married *someone to watch over me.*"

It was the day before her surgery and Tracey was as ready as anyone could be. Fellow Christians from all over the country were holding her up in prayer. She truly appreciated every prayer as well as the person praying it. She drew strength as well as encouragement from all the requests presented before God. She was living testimony that *prayer changes things.*

So many wanted to visit Tracey but I tried to keep the visitation to family and our closest friends. Our church announced from the pulpit that it was more important to pray for us than visit. Tracey asked me to allow only positive people to visit her. She didn't want anyone bringing her down with any negativity. She didn't want to see any sadness or crying and especially didn't want anyone feeling sorry for her. Tracey believed that selfish people looked for pity; she was looking for positive encouragement.

Her favorite visitor was Joey. He was two months away from his second birthday and oblivious to anything happening around him. He entertained his mommy as he ran around the hospital room creating havoc. Tracey would not allow me to discipline him during this time so Joey took full advantage of it.

Joey was the laughter in Tracey's voice and the smile inside her heart. He was the main reason for her fighting and beating this cancer. I wasn't allowed to even hug Tracey while she was in traction yet she had me put Joey in her arms so she could snuggle him. Somehow, he knew to lay still and not hurt mommy. No drug could comfort her more than holding her baby boy.

Later that day, I had an appointment with a representative from the hospital. I don't remember her name or even what she looked like; only what she had to say. She wanted to talk with me about the psychological effects the operation would have on our relationship. I was willing to listen, always wanting to be open to things that might benefit me.

She told me I needed to understand that Tracey was going into the operating room as one person and would exit as another. It would be impossible for things to be the same because Tracey was once a healthy young woman, but would now live the life of a woman with a handicap.

It was unfortunate that Tracey was so pretty. This would make the transformation even more devastating than if she had been unattractive. Now, when Tracey looks in the mirror she'll see the ugliness of her amputation, it will be hard for her to feel like a whole person again as she focuses more on what is missing from her life.

She continued to tell me Tracey would more than likely shun me physically so I needed to prepare myself for when she did. There was the possibility I might find myself feeling attracted to other women, but it would be a normal response.

It was her opinion that we should consider entering some kind of counseling so our marriage wouldn't fall apart. The trauma of the operation, along with the chemotherapy treatments, would be enough to send Tracey into a depression that could cause irreparable harm to our family. It would be very feasible Tracey would become a recluse.

I don't know why I allowed myself to listen to that garbage. Was that supposed to be my pep talk? Was I supposed to just give up and die? She presented herself as an expert in dealing with cancer patients, having a great deal of experience. However, I knew her advice stemmed from the lack of experience, an experience with Jesus.

The woman's advice might have benefited some, especially those not having a relationship with Jesus. Nevertheless, Tracey and I were walking with the Lord, trusting him with our marriage. Opinions found in some psychology book would not define our future. We weren't standing on some bridge contemplating whether to jump, no we were *standing on the promises* we found in God's word. Only a foolish man would choose the limited knowledge of man over the infinite wisdom of God.

The visiting hours were over. I decided to stay the night so I could be with Tracey up until surgery. We didn't talk much about the operation, trying to focus more on positive things; like Joey for example. Tracey started to tire and began nodding off a little. The room was quiet except for the usual sounds found in the halls of a hospital.

The chair I was trying to sleep in was the most uncomfortable thing I ever sat in. The vinyl covering made obnoxious sounds every time I attempted to move, I tried to be as still as possible so not to wake Tracey. I knew I was in for a long night and that horrible chair was only going to make it longer. I closed my eyes in an attempt to sleep. That's when Satan began his attack, big time.

The conversation I had earlier in the day was getting the best of me. I kept hearing that woman's words repeatedly inside my head. I started thinking, "What if she was right about Tracey? Will she ever really be the same? Will I walk into her room tomorrow and find some stranger? Is my marriage really over?"

I would almost jump from my chair as I wrestled with those thoughts. Every time I did, I would awaken Tracey.

She would look over and ask what was wrong. I just told her the stupid chair was uncomfortable and apologized for keeping her awake. I didn't want her to think I was worrying about the surgery. She had enough to worry about without adding me to her list. Before closing her eyes, she would say in earnest, "I'm going to be all right."

I would answer, "I know, I know."

The same thing kept happening well into the early hours of the morning. I kept sifting through all the trash dumped into my brain, starting to question whether I would even be able to take care of my family. Still, the constant squeaking of the chair kept stirring Tracey from her sleep.

Tracey never entered into a deep sleep. She was half-sleeping and half-praying; something I was trying to do. She must have said the words "I'm going to be all right" at least a dozen times. She knew my heart was breaking for her; she was more concerned that I was hurting than she was about sleeping. Somehow, Tracey wanted to let me know that she was really *going to be all right.*

After another loud squeak of the chair, Tracey opened her eyes and stared up at the ceiling. In a quiet, yet confident voice, she began to sing, *"Because He lives, I can face tomorrow. Because He lives, all fear is gone. Because I know, He holds the future. And life is worth the living just because He lives."*

Tracey glanced over at me just long enough for her eyes to find mine. She smiled briefly, and then went to sleep. There was nothing else to say or worry about. Only our hearts would sing those words throughout the night.

What was I thinking? How could I have possibly listened to all those lies knowing that God was in control? All night Tracey was trying to let me know that she could face tomorrow and all the tomorrows that would follow, just because He lives. Hope replaced her fears as she placed her future in the hands of her Savior.

Admittedly, her dreams might have been shattered, but she began to dream new ones. Living with one leg was not her main focus; *just living was*. The squeaking stopped, and the peace that passes all understanding filled the hospital room for the rest of the night.

BECAUSE HE LIVES

God sent His son -- they called Him Jesus,
He came to love, heal and forgive;
He lived and died to buy my pardon,
An empty grave is there to prove my Savior lives.

CHORUS:
Because He lives I can face tomorrow,
Because He lives all fear is gone;
Because I know He holds the future
And life is worth the living just because He lives.

How sweet to hold a newborn baby
And feel the pride and joy he gives;
But greater still the calm assurance:
This child can face uncertain days because Christ lives.

CHORUS

And then one day I'll cross the river,
I'll fight life's final war with pain;
And then as death gives way to victory,
I'll see the lights of glory and I'll know He reigns.

CHORUS

Chapter 2

Boy Meets Girl

I don't know what would have happened that night if Tracey and I didn't know Jesus. In fact, I'm not sure if I would have even been there. The counselor's words might have held true if our relationship with the Lord and each other was different. However, our dependence on God did not begin when Tracey found herself battling cancer. Our relationship with Jesus started many years before.

Tracey and I first met in 1979. I was on my way to preview a possible singing gig where a club owner contacted me to fill in for his vacationing singer. He offered me the job after hearing me sing at my own show across town. I thought I should check out the place before committing to work there.

I never had a singing lesson, didn't read a note of music, I just loved to sing. I would sing anywhere and to anyone who would listen. When I was a teenager, my dad bought me a reel-to-reel tape recorder to record myself singing. I would practice for hours, pretending I was a big star in Las Vegas but never considered singing as a career; then it was just for fun.

I got involved in nightclubs during my early twenties by accident. One night, I went with a group of people to a local nightspot where on Wednesday nights the club would present a take-off of the *Gong Show* seen on television. Each show was always fun and full of enjoyment.

A friend dared me to enter the contest, that's all it took to get me on stage. I sang a song that was popular at the time. Actually, it was the only song where I knew all the words. At the end of my performance, I received a standing ovation. I won the contest and was invited back week after week to perform with the house band. The owner eventually hired me and set aside a night for me to have my own show. This was the beginning of my new career.

I arrived at the place where I was to sing. I wasn't certain if I really wanted the job so I sat in the back trying not to be recognized. This way I'd just slip out if I decided it wasn't for me. The musicians were on a break so I ordered a beer and checked out the place.

While waiting, I spied a beautiful girl walking into the restaurant whose presence seemed to command everyone's attention. I thought, "My, my, who is that?" She had long dark hair and a gorgeous smile. The sparkle in her big brown eyes seemed to light up the room. There was a bounce in her walk, exuding confidence with every step. I likened her to a big ball of energy just waiting to explode.

My eyes followed her as she made her way toward the front. I wanted to see the lucky guy she was with but was surprised when she didn't sit down; she went right to the stage.

I said to myself, "This is the singer I'm filling in for; this is Tracey Chuchu."

I ordered another beer and waited anxiously to hear her sing. I started thinking, "This girl's good looking, but that doesn't mean she can sing. I'll be the judge of that."

When Tracey greeted the audience, she sounded like a sweet little girl more so than a mature woman. At first, I thought she was a little unprofessional, needing a few of my private lessons. However, I noticed the audience loved her approach and mirrored back the same warmth.

It became clear that Tracey was more than just a singer to them; they saw a daughter, a little sister, but mostly a friend. They were in the palm of her hand.

Again I thought, "Okay, she's beautiful and sweet, but can she sing?"

It was still early and the people were eating dinner, so the music would be a little softer during this set. Tracey acted very comfortable on stage, enjoying herself more than entertaining. I watched closely as I listened to her sing for the first time. Oh yea, she could sing, she could really sing. Her voice was just as beautiful as she was.

As I listened, I realized that there was something special and very different about her. However, I knew I'd probably have to get to know her to understand exactly what it was.

Tracey's song choice surprised me, a Gershwin song, *Someone to Watch Over Me*. She sang it beautifully but it was an old song for such a young singer. Still, I have to admit she sang it as though the composer wrote it especially for her.

Was she the old-fashioned type? Was she mature beyond her years? Whatever she was I could see that she was the real deal.

This was the first song I ever heard Tracey sing. Only time would reveal how the words would play out and how meaningful they would eventually be.

Someone to Watch Over Me
(Gershwin)

There's an old saying, says love that is blind
Still we're often told, "Seek and ye shall find"
So I'm going to seek a certain lad I've had in mind

Looking everywhere, haven't found him yet
He's the big affair I cannot forget
Only man I ever think of with regret

I'd like to add his initial to my monogram
Tell me, where is the shepherd for this lost little lamb?

There's a somebody I'm longing to see
I hope that he turns out to be
Someone who'll watch over me

I'm a little lamb who's lost in the wood
I know I could always be good to
One who'll watch over me

Although he may not be the man some girls think of as handsome
To my heart he carries the key!

Won't you tell him please to put on some speed
Follow my lead, oh, how I need
Someone to watch over me!

I enjoyed myself as the night progressed. Tracey had almost everyone dancing and singing along with her. Was I watching a nightclub singer or the *Pied Piper*? She actually had them doing the *Hokey Pokey*.

During her break, Tracey came over to my table to meet me. I realized early in our conversation that she was one of the nicest persons I had ever met. She sought no praise for her performance. She didn't need any attention from me; she had plenty already. She just wanted to thank me for filling in for her.

Unlike Tracey, I began to rattle on about myself. I bragged about my singing trying to convince her I was an undiscovered star. I was trying to impress her, never realizing how unimpressed she really was. I was convinced my voice was God's gift to the world. Unfortunately, I was the only one who was convinced.

Tracey just sat there and listened, and listened. Finally, she just burst out laughing right in my face.

I didn't remember saying anything deserving that kind of reaction so I asked, "What's so funny?"

She stood and started walking away. As she did I heard her mutter, "Oh nothing, jerk."

I couldn't believe it! I thought to myself, "Well, it was nice meeting you too, *Miss Thing*. Did she really call me a jerk? What did I say? What didn't I say? I thought I acted like a complete gentleman."

I didn't stay mad at her for very long. In fact, I was embarrassed, wishing I could start the conversation all over again. Some people call it "putting your foot in your mouth." It would have been better if I did, then I wouldn't have been able to talk at all. Oh well, I really didn't have to worry, it's not as if we had to work together.

I accepted the job and started the next weekend. The first night was slow. I was sure Tracey's fan club was boycotting the joint until she got back. They felt an allegiance to her for some reason. I would overhear people asking where she was or when she was coming back. I sang my heart out as always but didn't receive the same reception Tracey enjoyed. Some people didn't like me at all, requesting I turn down the volume.

It was quite humbling but I really didn't let it bother me. I just went to the bar during the breaks and pounded some beers. There was no sense talking to the crowd if they didn't appreciate good music when they heard it. At least the bartender liked me.

The crowd was more upbeat the following night. I was hoping to win them over finally. As usual, I arrived early enough to drink at the bar for a while. Under my facade of toughness and conceit was a very insecure young man. The booze gave me what I considered the missing ingredient I needed to relax and sing better, I called it my *liquid courage*. After enough drinks I could do or say anything, unfortunately I sometimes did. I didn't realize drinking was only masking my problems and inhibitions. The major accomplishment of drinking too much was not that I sang better, I could just puke with the best of them.

There are so many things in life that we use or do to try to cover up what we don't want to feel or have others see. Nevertheless, at this time in my life covering up seemed to work.

This night was definitely different. The people were starting to enjoy my music so I started to relax and even enjoy myself. After the dinner set we cranked up the volume and I let loose. Even Tracey's groupies started to like me.

However, the perfect night was about to change. Tracey strolled in with every head turning to greet her. The people actually started applauding. It was ridiculous!

Inside I was thinking, "What is she doing here? I thought I was here so she could go on vacation. Is she that mad at me for what I said, enough to come in and sabotage my night? Maybe this girl isn't as nice as I thought she was, maybe I underestimated her, maybe behind that shining smile lurks an *evil man-hater* who is out to make me hurt."

After finishing the set, I made my way straight to the booth where Tracey was sitting. Immediately, I asked her why she was there and not on vacation. She answered, "I am on vacation, vacation from work and singing."

Tracey worked a full-time day job and sang three nights a week in the club. She said she felt a little frazzled, needing some time just to do nothing. Going away on vacation sounded like work to her so she thought it might be relaxing to come out and hear some good music.

Right away, I knew Tracey wasn't still mad from the other night. She seemed like the kind of person that forgave without holding a grudge.

I said humbly, "Well, I hope you hear some good music tonight."

She said in response, "I'm sure I will, I hear the singer is pretty good."

I tried something different during that conversation. I talked more about Tracey instead of myself.

My break was over, time to get back on stage. I felt better about this conversation than I did the first time we talked. The only thing on my mind was to show Tracey how good I was.

When I returned, the piano player informed me that some of the patrons were asking if Tracey could sing.

I thought, "This is just great! If I say no, the crowd will think I'm jealous or egotistic. If I say yes, she'll probably steal the show. After all, I am in her house. This is definitely a no-win situation."

I agreed, but wasn't excited about the idea. However, Tracey showed just how classy she really was. To make sure she didn't steal the spotlight she suggested we sing a duet together.

I could only think, "What a nice, nice girl."

We both knew a ton of songs making it easy to choose something on the spot. As soon as the music started, nothing mattered except giving our best performance. There was no competition, in fact our voices blended so well together even we were amazed. Our eyes met briefly during the song as if to affirm we were good together.

When the music stopped, the people in the restaurant gave us a great ovation; our singing debut was a hit. It was a great ending to a shaky start.

I quit singing at the other nightclub a few months later. After hearing that I did, the owner where Tracey sang offered me a job. He thought it would be good for business to have both a male and female singer. Tracey was okay with the idea so it made the decision a no-brainer.

We formed a solid partnership as we continued to compliment one another's performance. Most notable was how tight our harmonies were; our duets became the crowd's most favorite thing.

As time went on, interacting with each other both on and off stage helped us improve our relationship with the audiences. In addition, performing together night after night drew us closer together as friends. Tracey began to see that the real Denny was not the same guy she first met. We were starting to be good friends but that would be as far as it would go.

One thing friends do is talk. Over a period of months, we would share many life experiences as well as stories about our families and friends. We were beginning to see just what made each other tick.

Tracey and I had very different personalities and characteristics. I was loud and boisterous; she was more reserved. She was conservative in her thinking and I was more on the liberal side. I demanded respect from others whereas she tried to earn it. People found me hard to accept but everyone loved Tracey. Getting into a fight or argument was very easy for me, while walking away and avoiding a confrontation was her choice. Celebrating and doing things to excess seemed far more fun to me than Tracey's mode of temperance.

We were two very different people. Music seemed to be the only thing we had in common.

Chapter 3

Just Friends

As time went on, Tracey and I saw the fruits of our effort. The restaurant was doing well as we continued to draw crowds to full capacity. The most important thing was having fun.

Singing was not making either of us rich. We both had other jobs to support ourselves. I worked as a commissioned salesperson at a major department store. I got my start in sales working for an independent men's clothier at the age of sixteen. The owner was a terrific boss, treating me more like a son than an employee. The education I received from this man was far greater than anything I learned from a textbook. He was a great salesman and successful entrepreneur. His example taught me how to interact with others and articulate when I spoke.

Tracey worked at Malone Advertising Agency where she hired in as a receptionist, having no background in advertising. However, they also realized there was something different about her. Tracey was always willing to go the extra mile. She not only did her job, but also was interested in helping others do theirs. People took notice and started involving her in other aspects of the business. Her willingness to work hard, coupled with the desire to learn, made her a more valuable employee.

Eventually, Tracey accepted the role of an associate media director, quite an accomplishment for an uneducated person. Tracey was living proof that although education opens doors, hard work will keep you there. Some of the most educated people fail in life because of their unwillingness to work hard and grow. *"Hard work will overcome talent when talent refuses to work hard."*- Jerry Schmidt.

We started many good friendships, but most significant was the friendship developing between the two of us. It was obvious we liked each other. Even Tracey had to admit there was something redeeming about me. We didn't date, but spent a lot of time together as friends.

Some nights after the restaurant closed, we would sit in the parking lot and talk until the sun came up. After realizing we had talked all night, we would go out for breakfast and continue the conversation. It's hard to spend that much time together without becoming involved with someone.

Tracey was different from other girls I knew. My interest in her was growing but it wasn't the usual attraction I experienced before. Sure, she was physically attractive, but there were better-looking girls in the world. There was more, something deeper and I wanted to get closer to whatever it was.

In time, I eventually expressed my desire to take our relationship to the next level. I let her know that she was very special to me. I thought of her as my best friend, feeling we had a good foundation to build upon.

Before meeting Tracey, I had relationships based on passion driven by physical attraction. Without hurting her feelings, I let her know I didn't think of her in the same way. I wanted something more substantial.

We were spending a lot of time together so it just seemed right to take the next step. It wasn't easy for me to allow myself to be vulnerable with my feelings. I thought she was worth it so I laid everything on the table.

I wasn't prepared for Tracey's response, although at least she began with some positive comments.

"Denny, I think you're very talented and I believe we're good together on stage. I feel you're a little too crazy at times but I still find you very funny. I enjoy being around you *most* of the time.

"I respect that you're so outspoken, although I don't always agree with you. I see that you have an inner strength that allows you to stand up for whatever you believe in, I admire that. And, well, I guess you're even a little cute.

"However, I can't allow myself to become deeply involved with you because of my relationship with Jesus. I'm sorry."

That's where it got confusing. I wasn't satisfied with her reasoning so I urged her to explain more in detail.

She said, "It's hard for me to explain, I'm not sure you'll understand."

"Just try me. I'm a lot smarter than you think."

Tracey replied, "I'm a Christian and I won't be involved with someone who's not. The Bible says that I am not to be *unequally yoked together with an unbeliever.*"

"Oh! Is that all you're worried about? I am a Christian. This is America isn't it? I believe in God just as much as the next guy."

I thought it rather presumptuous as well as rude of Tracey to suggest I didn't believe in God. Who did she think she was and how did she know what I believed in my heart? She hurt my feelings so I got mad.

"So, you think you're too good for me. If you're such a great Christian, why do you sing in a nightclub and why do you drink? What's up with all the make-up and those short skirts of yours? What makes you think you're better than I?"

I was on a roll. I don't remember all the things I said but the madder I got the longer the list grew.

Isn't it ironic how sometimes unbelievers can be more legalistic and demanding of Christians than the church? It might not be right or fair, but Christians do need to recognize that the world expects high standards from them.

Tracey confidently responded, "I don't think I'm better than you, I'm just better off."

You see, Tracey accepted Jesus as her personal Savior when she was a young teenager, however she was not spiritually mature enough to successfully witness to someone like me. It was obvious that I didn't comprehend what it really meant to be unequally yoked. Tracey wasn't being judgmental; she just realized I didn't understand what being a Christian really meant. I was more argumentative about religion than seeking it. She was learning how to walk the walk but still lacking in how to talk the talk. My personality was too confrontational for her at that time, therefore she felt inadequate to help me.

Tracey was struggling even more because her feelings for me were growing. She wanted me to understand the Gospel but knew she wasn't the one to reach me. It would take someone much bolder than Tracey to lead me to Jesus.

Tracey didn't want me to misunderstand and feel rejected. She shared an experience she had with the hopes of bringing more clarity to her stance concerning a Christian relationship.

Tracey started dating a fellow named David when she was a senior in high school. She described him as tall, dark, and handsome *of course*; one of the nicest guys you'd ever meet. As their relationship grew they fell very much in love.

One Christmas, David made it official by giving her a ring. They set a date for the wedding, ordered the invitations, and reserved a hall for the reception. Everyone believed this would be a marriage made in heaven, especially Tracey's mom. Shirley adored the young man and believed him to be perfect for her little girl.

Before getting married, they were required to attend premarital counseling at David's church. This is where Tracey's questioning began. Up to this point, there were no alarms concerning their relationship. She knew David belonged to a church of a different denomination than hers, but lacked a deeper understanding of what they believed. It was during these visits Tracey realized she could not go forward with the marriage.

There were many things Tracey couldn't agree with, she saw too many differences causing her to examine her own faith and dig deeper. As a born again believer Tracey realized that her understanding of salvation and the teachings of her church were too different from David's church. She told her mother she could never attend David's church and more importantly, would never agree to raise her children there.

Tracey told David of her decision and they went their separate ways.

After hearing Tracey's story, I still didn't understand why this religious stuff was so important to her. I thought I had some perception of God but obviously nothing as deep as she did. One thing was for sure, her beliefs were very strong and enough for me to back off. I figured if she wouldn't marry David, who sounded perfect, why would she have anything to do with me?

It didn't take me long to get over the anger and hurt. I admired Tracey even more and accepted her friendship as a gift. Through our conversations, I realized she had been making better decisions in life than I had. She believed deeply in what I was yet to find.

Chapter 4

The Star Doesn't Shine

One night, one of my work associates brought along a friend who was interested in hearing me sing. Apparently, he had some connections with a talent agent. At the end of the evening, he invited me to his table. Impressed by my singing, he asked if I ever thought of making it to the "big time." I told him it was a dream of mine but I didn't know where or how to begin.

He settled back into his chair, his eyes squinting from the smoke rolling off his big cigar. With a husky yet quiet voice he boldly said, "Son, I'm gonna make you a star, if you're willing to listen to me."

Things happened so fast it's really hard for me to remember all that happened. I eventually signed a contract with him, making him my new manager. I'm not sure how much I read, I was only concerned with the part about being famous.

He sent me to meet the booking agent he knew. He was one of the shadiest looking characters I had ever seen. He was all dressed in black and wearing dark sunglasses, looking like a cheap imitation of *Roy Orbison*. He epitomized the term "con artist." Every word that slithered out of his mouth sounded like a lie, even if it was the truth. After hearing me sing, he promised he would make me a famous.

I should have started running the moment I laid eyes on him except that he was my ticket to fame and fortune, so I stayed. I had no vision of right or wrong, good or bad, only of a dream to sing and make it big. I guess I was the one who needed the dark glasses along with a red tipped cane.

Then there was the question of what name I should go by. My last name is Kleibscheidel. Not one person thought it would look good in lights, let alone fit on a marquee. It really didn't bother me. All my life people either made fun of my last name or mispronounced it.

We spent a lot of time searching for a name. Some thought I should just use Denny while one reminded us you usually become famous before you're known by a single name. One fellow said, "Just look at the guy, there's nothing special about him, he looks like an *All-American guy*."

Ironically, my agent, who happened to be Jewish, suggested I use the name Denny Christian. "How much more American can you get than that?" he said laughingly.

Immediately, I said, "Yes! I love the name Christian." That settled it; my stage name would be Denny Christian.

I thought Tracey would surely be impressed if I used that name. She liked it but found it amusing that a Jewish man would suggest the name Christian. Looking back, I'm sure God was not impressed or amused that I was using this name. Although it wasn't the first time anyone used the name Christian without living out its meaning.

I must admit I was in my glory at first, so excited to see my name in lights. It was a thrill to drive into a new town and read the words, *"Now Appearing, Denny Christian."* It made me feel special but mostly proud. Sometimes I would stare at the marquee for the longest time while envisioning what it was going to look like in Las Vegas.

Yea, I was hooked, but not on drugs or anything similar. No, I was addicted to something far more deceptive and harmful, *self*.

At first this whole experience seemed to be a perpetual party. How much better could it be than to get paid for making music and having fun? The first thing I'd do at a new gig was negotiate free drinks for the band. It only took a couple of nights before the bartenders realized we were drinking them dry, then they would cut us off and start charging for what we drank.

I thought I needed the booze to help me be in front of people. Drinking made the people disappear, allowing me the freedom to perform without any inhibitions. I didn't realize how small you had to feel to "hide in a bottle."

As time went on, the luster of the lights started to fade. I rarely looked at the marquees except to see if they spelled my name right. Having my name in lights was more exciting when it was a *dream* than when it became a *reality*. This had become a job no longer fueled by the lust for fame. I questioned why this feeling set in before I made it big. How could anything start to get so old while it was still so new?

I didn't understand what was happening inside of me. At first, I thought it might be that I missed Tracey. Our time apart made us both realize we were starting to fall in love. However, those feelings weren't from missing someone, I've done that before and got over it. No, these were stranger feelings. My life was missing something but it wasn't Tracey.

One night I walked to a neighborhood bar to unwind after our last set. The place was a real dive but I wasn't looking for ambience, just a place to be alone. At least it was quiet, just what I needed after hearing a few hundred watts of electric guitar and drums beating in my ear.

The place was empty except for the bartender and a little old man sitting at the end of the bar. I ordered a scotch on the rocks, top shelf of course, then glanced over at the old man and raised my glass to him. He ignored my gesture so I continued to stare straight ahead minding my own business.

After a while, the silence was interrupted by the old man's begging for a free drink. The bartender reached down under the bar for a bottle, either his own stash or some cheap bar whiskey. As he poured the drink he would say, "This is the last one, you've had enough. You need to go home."

That didn't stop the old man from continuing to beg. After much pleading, the bartender would give in filling his glass several more times while repeating the same words, "You've had enough. You need to go home."

The old man just ignored what the bartender was saying, probably because he had no home to go to; that barstool was home to him.

Finally, the bartender stood his ground and refused to give him anymore. I felt sorry for the old guy but at the same time irritated by his crying for more. To keep him quiet I told the bartender to give him a drink and put it on my tab. He served up the drink but the old man never looked my way to thank me or even acknowledge where it came from. But it didn't really matter where it came from or where it would lead. *It was one more drink.*

His hands began to shake as he reached carefully for the drink. He forced his lips to the glass making sure not to spill even a drop. Once when he dripped a bit onto the bar he leaned over and lapped it up with his tongue.

I started to really pity the old man while thinking, "This poor guy. Here I am all cleaned up in a tuxedo while he wears tattered clothes, smelling like a sewer. I just received the applause of hundreds of people while no one cares if he's even alive. I have a roll of money in my pocket able to afford top shelf while this poor sap can only beg for cheap whiskey. I'm living out my dream while he's dying in his nightmare."

Soon my thoughts began to change, the pity I was feeling for the old man turned to cold fear. The next time when I looked at him it was as if I saw myself sitting there. I was that old man; that was my future, my nightmare. The outward appearance no longer made a difference.

For the first time in my life, I realized I was just as poor and lost as that old man was. It no longer mattered what the content of the bottle was, we were still drinking from the same cup, headed in the same direction that led to ruin. I felt an indescribable void in my heart with no end to its emptiness.

The bartender's words kept resonating through my head, "You've had enough. It's time to go home."

I threw money on the bar and ran from that place until it was no longer in sight. My mind was filled with so many confusing questions. "Why was this happening to me? What do I need to do? Where should I go? Most of all, how do I make sure I don't end up like that old man?"

As I approached the hotel where I was performing, I looked up at my name on the marquee. I thought, "Yea, big deal! Instead of Denny Christian it should read Denny the Loser." Ironically, the timer clicked and the power went off, the sign bearing my name went dark; a fitting end to this crazy night.

A better ending would have read something like this: I ran to my room, fell on my knees, and asked God to save me. Unfortunately, that never happened. I didn't know how to pray or what it meant to be saved. I'm sure I passed by many Christians in my life without anyone sharing the "plan of salvation" with me. At least Tracey was still trying.

It wasn't long before the lights faded completely. I knew the road I was traveling on would never lead to what I actually needed. Ending up like that old man was far from what I dreamed for myself. There had to be something better in life and I was resolved to find it, knowing somehow Tracey would help me.

Chapter 5

Invite That Boy to Church

I was invited back to sing with Tracey. It seemed like I'd never left although some things were different, or should I say something was different about me? It was hard to enjoy myself and get back into singing. I was no longer on the road but there was still a constant unrest in my soul. My search for the reasons why was consuming me.

Tracey and I were growing very close even against her better judgment. She was struggling with a big dilemma. She was attracted to the same person whom she felt was so unappealing. So why was she drawn to me? It wasn't so much what she saw in me but how I made her feel.

It was now winter and the nights were very cold. After closing, Tracey and I would stand out in the parking lot and talk for hours. One night Tracey's body began to shiver while her teeth started to chatter.

I put my arms around her to protect her from the cold, holding as tight as possible without hurting her. She told me my arms felt strong and made her feel warm and secure. I responded by telling her what a good arm wrestler I was and proceeded to share some stories of my most exciting matches. I didn't get many words out before Tracey stopped me. She was not impressed or interested in hearing another of my testosterone-filled stories. She was referring to an emotional feeling, not anything physical.

Tracey felt safe and protected when I held her in my arms. While we stood there, I reminded her of the first song I heard her sing, *Someone to Watch Over Me*. I asked if she wanted me to be like the fellow in the song and watch over her. She acknowledged the possibility.

Tracey was struggling with her feelings. She knew it was wrong to start a relationship with this unbeliever and contrary to what the Bible taught. *"Do not be yoked together with unbelievers...What does a believer have in common with an unbeliever?"* (2 Corinthians 6:14)

This illustration was used to show that although opposites might attract, they don't necessarily walk in the same direction. They should only allow themselves to be yoked together, *especially intimately*, with those who are walking in the same light and direction as they are. It is not only painful but also sometimes futile to try otherwise.

Surely, I could not be the person God would choose for Tracey. As she attempted to repent for falling in love with me, the Lord interrupted by admonishing her to get me to church. She was reluctant to obey at first, questioning why God would want her to take me to church. Still, she felt in her spirit that God wanted me in church and she was the one who could get me there.

Tracey was the song leader of a conservative holiness church, a *Free Methodist Church*, so I'm sure she felt embarrassed to take me. How could she sneak someone like me in without notice? She knew without a doubt that there was no hiding Denny, I would stand out like a sore thumb, smelling like a brewery from the night before. She knew when the music started my big bellowing voice would drown out the whole congregation, announcing that Denny was in the house.

God was persistent. Tracey could almost hear him say, "Invite that boy to church."

"But Lord, he's no one I would ever pick for myself."

"Invite that boy to church."

"But Lord, I really don't think he's that cute."

"Invite that boy to church."

"But Lord, we're just friends having a good time."

"Invite that boy to church."

"But Lord, he drinks and smokes too much."

"Don't worry, you invite him, I'll clean him up."

Tracey decided she had to either cut all ties with me or invite me to church. God wanted to be involved with whomever she was involved with. He wanted what was best for Tracey and I was already part of his plan for her life. She allowed me to enter her heart; therefore, God would show her what to do the rest of the way. He gave her eyes to see not only who I was but also who I could be with Jesus sitting on the throne of my life.

Tracey began to talk more about how great her church was and even more about how Jesus changed her life. I thought it was great Tracey felt like this, although the more I listened the more I thought I might be getting in over my head. I started to think, "Maybe I wasn't good enough for this girl. Maybe she deserved a nicer guy, some church guy." Being with her didn't always make me feel good about myself; her life seemed to point out all of my flaws. I was overcome by low self-esteem and felt as though I didn't measure up. I was afraid Tracey was trying to change me into someone I didn't want to be, or even could be.

Tracey kept saying many wonderful and positive things although I didn't always understand. I believed in God and used to pray before I went to bed each night, *Now I Lay Me Down to Sleep*. I didn't know all the "spiritual lingo" but I did understand what I saw with my eyes. I saw a girl that always brought a light into a darkened situation, who always had a positive attitude when there was every reason to be negative. I saw a girl who was amazingly talented but gave all the credit to God. I decided that if she invited me to go to her church, I would go.

It was now early January of 1980, time for Tracey to take me to church. When she first asked me to go, she was a little surprised at my eagerness to attend. I'm sure she was elated to think that I was acquiring some great hunger for God although the only real hunger I had was for our relationship to get to the next level.

I didn't exactly understand what made Tracey tick. However, through our conversations I did realize there were three things that had to happen before we could seal the deal. I was sure I could handle at least two out of the three.

First, there was an obvious physical attraction. Right or wrong, most people will never get to know someone if they don't pass the eye test. That was not a problem.

Second, we made each other feel good when we were together. Singing the words of a love song touched our hearts in a way no normal conversations could have. We shared many laughs together as well as tears so I felt confident the emotional part was also satisfied.

There's a song that says, *"Two out of three aint bad."* Having a relationship with an attractive person who at the same time makes you feel good, what more could you ask for. To the world, it might have been plenty, but Tracey was asking for more. Two out of three was not good enough; the *spiritual ingredient* of the relationship was missing. God needed to be the third partner in the relationship; he needed to be the one who would yoke us together. I realized this so I was willing to go to church, searching not so much for God, but to win Tracey over completely.

It wasn't going to be hard for me to walk into Tracey's church. I considered myself to be in the category of believers. I knew I wasn't atheist or agnostic. I never questioned the existence of God or demanded some kind of material proof. I thought I was a good guy, just a little rough around the edges maybe.

It was somewhat comical to me when people referred to me as a heathen. I didn't murder anyone or even steal while growing up. I treated people fairly as long as they did me. There were people far more evil in the world than I. In fact, I knew some people who went to church that were meaner than I was.

I was sure I never did anything bad enough for God to send me to hell. I remember reading a story in high school of how God threw Lucifer into hell because of his rebellion. I didn't feel like I was rebelling against God, at least consciously. Anyways, I always heard that God was a "God of love" so I couldn't believe a loving God could destroy his children in a "lake of fire." I wasn't perfect and I knew nobody else was, so I was willing to let God help me with some of the hurts and flaws I had. Maybe that's what Tracey wanted for me.

In the days leading up to Sunday, Tracey started prepping me for the experience. She wanted to make sure I knew what to expect, probably so I wouldn't suffer any from culture shock. She warned me most everyone had adopted her and might be somewhat protective of her. More importantly, she was making sure I was going to behave myself and not embarrass her. I assured her there was nothing to worry about.

I had this whole thing under control. After a little snooping, I found out a little about her church and was determined not to let those "holy rollers" intimidate me. I told Tracey I intended to sit right up front, not with the sinners in the back of the church. She knew how ornery I was so her usual response was a fake smile accompanied with a slight shaking of the head. She thought I was funny but tried not to encourage me.

Now, this brings us to the "Right Reverend Charles Young." I had been hearing about this guy for a lot longer than I ever wanted to hear about anyone. All Tracey could talk about was "Charlie this, and Charlie that." as well as "My pastor is nicest man I've ever met. He is so smart and such a powerful speaker. He and his wife Brenda are the nicest couple I have ever met."

I hated this guy and I hadn't even met him yet.

Was she crazy? Didn't she know that guys who have low self-esteem are very jealous and can't stand to have someone they love praise some other fellow? I couldn't wait to see this pastor and maybe get my hands on him. We'll see "who's the man!"

Chapter 6

No Surrender

*T*racey's invitation to accompany her to church was monumental to our relationship. In my mind, she was saying she wanted me as much as I wanted her. Although in reality, she was hoping I would want Jesus as much as he wanted me.

As we entered the church, there was a stirring of people moving from their Sunday school classes to the sanctuary. Everyone had to stop and talk to Tracey. It was obvious she was the same *little princess* at this church as she was at the nightclub. When she introduced me, many people acknowledged they had already heard about me. They welcomed me, expressing that they were pleased to meet me and glad I was there. They were living proof that "white man do talk with fork-ed tongue."

Don't get me wrong, I would never accuse those gracious people of lying. However, what they were really thinking was Tracey had completely backslidden and lost her mind. Each one was ready to defend their precious little girl from the "big bad wolf." They were glad I was there, and knew I needed to be, but just not with Tracey. I was aware of their apprehension toward me and was determined to make them like me. I was afraid if they didn't accept me it might negatively influence Tracey. The church handout should have read, *Welcome Sinner, Just Stay Away From the Song Leader.*

Tracey asked where I wanted to sit, so I told her right up front where the action is. I was very comfortable as we walked toward the front pew. Tracey on the other hand was curiously nervous. She had many quirks about her, always twitching her nose, or her hands and shoulders. She was always in constant motion, even more pronounced when she was nervous or excited. I never saw her this bad at the nightclub. Maybe church people are worse critics than the ones at the club. I told her not to worry. I knew how to take care of the hecklers. She said, "You worry me, not them!"

I sat down as she went up on the platform to sit with the pastor. As the music started, people began making their way to their seats. They were very friendly, greeting one another with hugs and smiles. Everyone seemed happy to be there while at the same time showing a level of respect and reverence for where they were. Many went out of their way to greet me with a genuine hand of friendship.

It made sense why Tracey was at this church; they were family. She fit in despite how conservative they seemed. In fact, I didn't notice anyone other than Tracey wearing makeup. They accepted her just the way she was.

The music stopped, drawing my attention towards the front. Pastor Charlie, the man himself, stood behind the pulpit exclaiming with a strong and robust voice, "This is the day that the Lord hath made, let us rejoice and be glad in it. Please stand, as we pray for God's blessing on our service this morning."

He began to pray and boy did he pray! I never heard anything so long. How could he think of all those things to say? I knew we were in trouble. If he could pray that long, his sermons must go on forever. Tracey didn't warn me to bring a sack lunch. He had us sit down while he shared the morning announcements. I wasn't really interested so I took this time to size him up.

Are you kidding me? This can't be the same person Tracey has been bragging about. All right, I will concede there wasn't anything wrong with him, but what was so special? I sure didn't see it. He was twenty-six years old, the same age as me. How could a man that young be any good? I thought a good preacher had to at least be seventy or so and do nothing but scream, "You're all going to hell!"

He was an "average looking Joe," no *Brad Pitt* by any means. He wore a smile on his face most of the time and when he did smile, you couldn't see his eyes. There was something likeable in his voice, a certain inflection I couldn't place. He just sounded like a good 'ole boy. There was nothing so far to make me think he was the next Billy Graham but I thought I would at least give him a chance.

I found out later that Charlie had grown up in French Lick, Indiana, explaining the way he sounded. He and his family eventually moved to Ohio where he accepted Jesus as his savior. His pastor was Dr. John Maxwell, one of the country's prominent authorities on church growth and leadership. Charlie was John Maxwell's very first convert to enter into full-time ministry. John affectionately referred to Charlie as his "preacher boy."

I saw his wife Brenda for the first time when she was inviting all the children to go forward for Children's Moments. She reminded me of Tracey because of the same godly glow about her. I could tell by the way she spoke that she was very intelligent and seemed so genuine. Her way of communicating with the children was very unique. They couldn't help but to hang on her every word.

As I looked around the congregation, I noticed every adult assuming the same posture, having the same receptive ear. Brenda's message about Jesus was simple enough for the children to grasp but contained a profound meaning for someone like me to process.

When it came time for the song service, Tracey bounced, literally, into place and led everyone in the congregational singing. It was somewhat strange listening to her. She was a low alto and the songs were not in her key. It made me chuckle when she had to switch to a falsetto voice to hit the high soprano notes, although I'm sure very few knew the difference. The most important thing was she loved what she was doing.

We sang only hymns. There were no contemporary praise songs, only some of the most anointed songs ever written. I didn't know most of the songs but I was able to pick up the melody by the second verse. As we sang, the words seemed to leap off the pages and go straight to my heart. Now I understand that the Holy Spirit was using the music to soften hearts and open minds for the Word to enter.

We did sing one song I was familiar with, *Amazing Grace*. This song was so meaningful I remember singing out at the top of my voice. Nevertheless, my fervor started to dissipate and my voice quieted as I applied the words to my own life. *"Amazing Grace how sweet the sound that saved a wretch like me. I once was lost, but now am found, was blind, but now I see."* As beautiful as those words were, they served to remind me that I was lost and blind, still a *wretched* soul.

After the singing, Pastor Charlie made his way to the pulpit. After reading a verse from the Bible, he began to preach. I had decided before getting there that this is when I would probably nap. I didn't expect to understand what would be said since I didn't regularly attend. Anyways, I was there to impress Tracey.

I sat back with my arms folded across my chest, almost daring Tracey's *hero* to say something impressive. From the moment he spoke, I realized there was something extraordinary about this fellow. It seemed as though the words coming from his mouth had something *seasoning or sweetening* them before entering my ears. It was like taking a deep breath of your favorite food; the aroma spreads throughout the cavities of your head making its way into your stomach. I didn't know the terminology then but this pastor's sermon was anointed.

As I continued to listen, I forgot all about Tracey and my original motives for even going. I uncrossed my arms and leaned forward with my elbows on my knees. I listened intently to what the man of God was saying and was able to understand every word he spoke. He preached in a way even a sinner like me could understand. I felt no reason to doubt that what he preached was truth. I don't remember what the exact sermon was but I do remember he was a long-winded preacher. When the sermon was over, I was still hungry for more.

Pastor Charlie had everyone stand at the end of his sermon. Tracey led the congregation in a song entitled *I Surrender All*. While we sang, several people went forward and kneeled at the altar. I felt good for those people even without knowing them. It was touching but at the same time very sobering. I had no idea what they were praying for but it made me think, "Maybe one day I might be able to surrender all. I just need to know more." I found myself already looking forward to next Sunday.

When we got to the car, I asked Tracey if she could drive. I felt somewhat weak, like I'd been beaten up in a fight. Tracey was concerned, hoping I wasn't turned off by the service. I assured her I enjoyed it very much but the whole experience seemed to magnify the void I had in my heart.

The battle for my soul had just begun.

Chapter 7

Just As I Am

The days and weeks that followed were adventuresome. No, I didn't go anywhere exciting, but I was on somewhat of a *treasure hunt* searching for the truth. I was determined to see what Tracey saw, feel what she felt, and have what she had. I was not going to be left out or left behind.

My whole life was similar to a "big puzzle" with a variety of people helping to fit the pieces together. Tracey was the *shining light* that attracted me in the first place. Pastor Charlie was preaching the *Living Word* that was coming alive in me. Brenda was the *illustrator*, helping to simplify even the most difficult questions.

However, the most important one helping was the person of Jesus. Everyone and everything was leading me to him. I was getting to know about Jesus. The more I did the closer I came to finding my treasure.

On the first Sunday of February, I went to church with enough understanding to help me make the greatest decision of my life. I knew if I heard God speak to me in the service, if I felt any tug by the Holy Spirit, I was going to surrender. I prepared my heart for this moment by all that I absorbed through seeing the Word lived out, hearing the Word preached, and comprehending the Word as I read it. The Word is the Bible.

I understood that Jesus came to earth as God incarnate; Jesus was God with *flesh on him*. He came to fulfill prophecy, to give purpose to it and reveal its truth. However, Jesus didn't come to enforce the law or to condemn the world. He came to save it by dying for our sins, even mine.

I also realized that I was a sinner and separated from God. *"...for all have sinned and fall short of the glory of God,"* (Romans 3:23) Jesus took my sin upon himself and nailed it to a cross, dying for me. It cost me nothing; it cost him everything. *"But God demonstrates his own love for us in this: While we were still sinners, Christ died for us."* (Romans 5:8)

Nevertheless, there was still a big question. How can there be so many different religions in the world? Which one should I choose? If Christianity was true, are all the other religions untrue? This was a legitimate question and very hard for someone like me to understand, let alone answer.

I heard so many people say that just believing in a god was enough, it doesn't matter what you call him. On the other hand, so many others claim their religions are the only way and are even willing to die for it. The Bible says I only get one chance on earth to make the correct decision. *"Just as man is destined to die once, and after that to face judgment, so Christ was sacrificed once to take away the sins of many..."* (Hebrews 9:27)

The *Bible* says, *"For the message of the cross is foolishness to those who are perishing, but to us who are being saved it is the power of God."* (1 Corinthians 1:18) *"For the time will come when men will not put up with sound doctrine...They will turn their ears away from the truth and turn aside to myths."* (2 Timothy 4:3)

All religions seem to have some benefits and do contain some truth, but I wanted the "whole truth and nothing but the truth."

Jesus claimed to be God. He said, *"I am the way and the truth and the life. No one comes to the Father except through me."* (John 14:6) He also said, *"I and the Father are one."* (John 10:30) Jesus validated his own *deity* by his own words, his miracles, death and resurrection.

By His claims I could only conclude that Jesus was either lying, out of his mind or he was who he said he was, God. I could not understand how so many religions accept Jesus as a great prophet, but reject him as God. How could you revere a man if he was a *liar or crazy*? I chose to believe Jesus was God. It was obvious to me that other teachings were religions about a god; Christianity was a relationship with God.

It was time for the service to begin so I got into my normal position, sitting close to the front with my elbows on my knees. I realized what Jesus did for me but what was I supposed to do? Somehow, I needed all this head knowledge to come to life.

I'm convinced God planned the message that morning just for me. Pastor Charlie talked about being *born again*, starting his sermon with the words, "Jesus spoke to Nicodemus, *'I tell you the truth, unless a man is born again, he cannot see the kingdom of God.... You must be born again.'* (John 3:3-7)

"It's not starting all over physically, but a *spiritual rebirth.* *'Therefore, if anyone is in Christ, he is a new creation; the old has gone, the new has come!'* (2 Corinthians 5:17)"

It still seemed hard to understand. How would I start my life all over again and be a new creature?

Pastor Charlie explained. "The transformation is similar to the metamorphosis of a caterpillar. The caterpillar spins its cocoon, while inside it completely changes, emerging as a beautiful butterfly. Having Christ come into your life allows the *sinful man* to die and the *righteous man* to emerge, only it is not the man's righteousness, it is God's."

As I sat there, I saw myself living in a cocoon or tomb, dead in my sins and trying to get out.

I thought, "But how do I get out? What do I have to do to change?"

Pastor Charlie continued, "You can do nothing to save yourself from sin. The Bible says, *'For it is by grace you have been saved, through faith—and this not from yourselves, it is the gift of God— not by works, so that no one can boast.'* (Ephesians 2:8)

"Being a good man isn't enough. You could do "good works" every day for the rest of your life and it still would not get you in to Heaven. Joining a church and attending every Sunday without fail will not save you from your sin for you are saved only by grace; grace being *unmerited favor*. This means you don't get what you deserve at the end of life, which is Hell; you get what you don't deserve, which is Heaven.

"It is like a condemned man sitting on death row. He is totally guilty and deserving of death but receives a pardon from the judge, sparing his life. God, the Eternal Judge pardons us from our sin because Jesus paid the penalty for our guilt when he died on the cross.

"To be born again you have to *believe* Jesus came to earth to die for our sins, that through him and only him we can have eternal life. *'For God so loved the world that he gave his one and only Son, that whoever believes in Him will not perish, but have eternal life.'* (John 3:16)

"However, just believing is not enough. Even the demons in hell believe. You must also *confess* your sins. *'If we confess our sins, he is faithful and just and will forgive us our sins and purify us from all unrighteousness.'* (1 John 1:9) When we confess, we're not telling God anything he doesn't already know. Confession is telling God we acknowledge that we are responsible for our own sin and no one else. We cannot fault our parents or society; we cannot use some bad experience or our position in life as a reason to sin. We admit there is no excuse and we accept total blame, seeking God's forgiveness.

"Confessing our sin is not complete without *repentance*. Many men will confess their sins but continue to hold on to them. Repentance is being sorry for your sins, enough to turn away from them. It means to do an about face, changing the direction you walk and the way you think.

"Once you were walking away from God toward sin and destruction; repentance turns you back around toward God and eternal life. *'Godly sorrow brings repentance that leads to salvation and leaves no regret, but worldly sorrow brings death.'* (2 Corinthians 7:10) Worldly sorrow is saying you are sorry but *not willing to change*, continuing to do the same things.

"You need to *receive* Jesus as Savior. *'Yet to all who received him, to those who believed in his name, he gave the right to become the children of God.'* (John 1:12) You need to invite Jesus to come into your life and take up residency. God gave man a *free will* to choose for himself whether to accept or reject him. Jesus is gently knocking at the door of your heart, but only you can open it for him to come in. He wants to have an intimate, personal relationship with you.

"He's more than the "big man in the sky"; He's not some "good ole' boy" as so many refer to him. He is a holy God and wants you to share in his holiness. *'Make every effort to live in peace with all men and to be holy; without holiness no one will see the Lord.'* (Hebrews 12:14)

"In the heart of every man is a throne. Whoever sits on that throne is the lord of everything in that person's life. Every thought and every action is controlled by whoever is lord. Receiving Jesus as your personal savior results in you stepping down and allowing him to sit on the throne of your life. Jesus becomes not only your savior, but also your Lord."

Pastor Charlie concluded by saying, "Jesus said to his disciples, *'If anyone would come after me, he must deny himself and take up his cross and follow me. For whoever wants to save his life will lose it, but whoever loses his life for me will find it. What good will it be for a man if he gains the whole world, yet forfeits his soul?'* (Matthew 16:24-26)

I realized there was a cost to following Jesus, but the cost would be nothing compared to what he was willing to pay. I would have to deny myself and take up my cross daily. I'm sure as I followed I would realize more of what that meant and what my cross might contain.

I finally realized that God does not send anyone to hell; they choose to go by refusing to follow Jesus.

The most important thing was I would be following Jesus into a glorious life, both here and eternal. For Jesus said, *"I have come that they may have life, and have it to the full."* (John 10:10) I tried the world and it didn't offer anything comparable.

I felt as though I had *new eyes*. I originally came to church with my eyes fixed on a pretty girl only to have them move onto a young pastor as he spoke so boldly. However, this day my eyes left that "preacher man" and for the first time, I saw Jesus, nailed to cross, dying for me.

We stood to sing after Pastor Charlie finished with his message. He invited anyone who wanted to accept Jesus to come forward. I heard God speaking to me loud and clear through his servant during the service, I was ready.

The organist started to play the introduction to the invitation, *Just As I Am*. I had already decided I would move out of my pew the instant the first word was sung, *except I didn't*. My feet would not move; they felt nailed to the floor, so I just sang, *"Just as I am without one plea, but that Thy blood was shed for me. And that Thou bidst me come to thee, Oh Lamb of God I come, I come."*

Satan was pulling out all stops. He was fighting for my soul, filling me with doubts and fears to keep me from making a decision for Christ. I looked ahead at the next verse that read *"Just as I am and waiting not, to rid my soul of one dark blot. To Thee whose blood can cleanse each spot, Oh Lamb of God I come, I come."*

I remembered a verse Pastor Charlie quoted in an earlier service, *"Today, if you hear his voice, do not harden your hearts..."* (Hebrews 3:15) I would not wait another moment. I would not be ashamed to step out in front of all those people for I was more ashamed to stay in my pew, a sinner.

As we began to sing the second verse, I threw my hymnal down on the pew and ran to the altar. I began to tremble while tears streamed from my eyes. All I kept saying inside was "Jesus, I am so, so sorry. Please, please forgive me. I am such a sinner."

I felt such tremendous shame, such unworthiness. I continued to sob as I kept placing more and more onto the altar, I was not going to leave without knowing I was forgiven.

Pastor Charlie knelt down on the other side of the altar asking, "Hey brother, what do want God to do for you today?"

I answered, "I want Jesus to save me from my sins."

He invited me to pray along with him, *"Dear Jesus, I confess that I am a sinner in need of a savior. I know that I deserve the consequences of my sin, yet I believe that you died for my sin so I could have eternal life. Please come in and be my personal Lord and Savior. Thank you for saving me, thank you for forgiving me! Amen!"*

Before I left the altar, Pastor Charlie hugged me and told me he was proud of me. I didn't know him very well, yet I already loved him like a brother. I tarried at the altar for a while just to make sure all was settled.

As everything started to sink in, I felt an overflow of different emotions. I felt drained, as though I just had my stomach pumped to remove some deadly drug. It was better than the release I felt after finally confessing to wrecking my dad's car; more liberating than having a deep, dark secret finally exposed and brought into the light. Mostly, it was seeing me break away from the clutches of sin, only to be held in the arms of a loving Father.

After a while, I could feel the color returning to my face along with my heart rate settling back to normal. My clothes were damp and I felt clammy all over. My eyes were swollen and bloodshot but I really didn't care. I might have looked frazzled on the outside, but I had a real sense of calm and peace on the inside. Not all people have the same kind of experience when they come to Christ; mine was very emotional.

Tracey was elated, but not surprised; she knew it was going to happen. It was what she was praying for all along.

I did most of the talking as we drove home from church. I wanted to let her know what happened at the altar and what I was thinking. Happy tears filled her eyes as she looked upon her new Denny.

What happened was all so ironic. One day I'm getting a standing ovation for singing in a nightclub. The next, all the angels in heaven are celebrating and cheering for me; a sinner has come home. My biggest dream was to have my name in lights, but God's vision was to have my name in the *Lamb's Book of Life*.

I would no longer be known as Denny Christian, but Denny, "a Christian."

Chapter 8

From This Day On

I finally found the treasure I had been searching for, salvation. However as I continued to look into God's "treasure chest" I realized there was so much more he wanted me to discover. I recognized that my mission was not over but just beginning.

I accepted Jesus by faith and resolved myself to walk the rest of the way by faith. I never awakened any morning doubting what had happened was real. I believed God totally for his promises or I would have never made the decision. A song says, *"I have decided to follow Jesus...no turning back, no turning back."* My new life would be full of many questions, but questions are not necessarily synonymous with doubt. I would never doubt my salvation, but would question where it was going to lead me.

I was not searching for "loopholes to sin"; spending time trying to figure out what part of my old life was still permissible. Rather, I was seeking to do the things that would be pleasing to God so I could be what he wanted me to be. I was sitting under a ministry challenging me to be more like Jesus. The result of that would be to live a holy life. The more willing I was to follow Jesus, the closer I got to him. I began to let go of the things that once seemed important to me only to grasp on to what was essential to God.

One of the first challenges came on a Wednesday night a few weeks after I was saved. Tracey and I were talking at the nightclub while on a break. I didn't feel like being there because I felt we should be at Bible Study instead of singing in a bar.

Up until then, Tracey never felt convicted of singing in a secular nightclub. The church didn't support her being there but wasn't challenging her to quit either. She was consistently growing so everyone trusted that God would let her know when to stop. Anyway, how would we have ever met if she had quit? More importantly, how would I have met Jesus? Sometimes God puts us in places the church would never think of going.

It didn't take very long for me to assume the spiritual leadership in our relationship. Now our lives were going to start changing rapidly.

Tracey agreed it was probably more important to be in church that night but there wasn't anything we could do about it right then; I saw things differently. I was now a Christian but still the same impulsive Denny, just redirecting my thoughts and energies.

Tracey and I were singing a duet during the last set of the evening when I lost all composure right in the middle of the song. I threw my microphone onto the floor and walked off stage yelling, "I can't do this anymore!" Everything stopped and no one said anything. Fortunately, it was a slow night so not too many had to experience my outburst. Tracey was mortified and embarrassed. She was so mad at me and sure let me have it. The owner's wife started to cry, I felt like the biggest loser.

I put no thought into my actions. I reacted to how I was feeling with no regard to the feelings of others. I was so wrong and could only apologize as I calmly tried to explain the motivation behind what I did. What were they supposed to think? Okay, this guy acted like a crazed maniac because he wanted to be in church? Agreeably, I was not the greatest witness.

We agreed to finish out the week, ending our secular career.

Tracey didn't stay mad at me for very long. She saw my outbursts before and realized there would likely be more. I was just trying to purge myself from anything that might get in the way of being able to grow. I did not believe God wanted us to be in that environment anymore. My methods were wrong but my motives were right.

Tracey and I continued to search for the deeper things of God. It was a process. As God showed us areas needing attention, we would attempt to be obedient by allowing him to work in our lives. We knew that only through the power of the Holy Spirit could we ever hope to live up to the expectations God had for us.

Seeking to get closer to God led us into a deeper relationship with each other. We were on a similar journey with similar goals. Although a relationship with God is personal, it seemed as though he wanted us to be together to work as a team. God had a purpose for our lives that involved each other; our conversations led us to the subject of marriage.

This is where the story is supposed to get all mushy and romantic. I'm sure it would be good reading if I said our deep burning passion for one another was so intense I whisked Tracey off to Paris and eloped. Or how 'bout this, I took her to the most expensive restaurant in town where I proposed by candlelight surrounded by a dozen violinists playing Italian love songs. How about something for you sports fans, I took her to a professional ball game and had the words "Will you marry me, Tracey" written on the side of a blimp.

Disappointing as it may be, none of those things happened. Actually, there was no particular day we considered as the day of engagement, in fact I never officially proposed to Tracey. Our discussions about our future led to a mutual understanding that we should get married so she never owned an engagement ring. We decided the engagement thing was something we would bypass and just get married.

Ours was not some passionate love affair fueled by raging hormones. We weren't looking for explosions to happen every time we kissed. We never uttered the words, "I can't live without you." I've already shared that I experienced relationships before where such words were spoken and found out that I could live without them and was better off doing so. Our relationship was deeper because we were a team, a partnership, and a couple of best friends enjoying each other's company.

Jesus' model of true love was what we wanted for our marriage. A love that was sacrificial and unselfish, putting each other's needs and desires ahead of our own. Jesus came to serve, not to be served; He was a giver, not a taker. That's what we wanted to imitate.

Tracey and I knew our wedding day would be cause for celebration. The more we talked about it the more excited we got. However, we solemnly considered the steps we were taking and tried to think beyond that day. We wanted to think that even the most uneventful day of our marriage should contain just as much love and joy as our wedding day. Making one day more important than another could set us up for disappointment; finding ourselves singing *The Thrill is Gone*. We wanted to place our feet on the level ground of consistency, and then we could celebrate on the mountaintops and survive in the valleys. We decided to sing this "song of life" as a duet.

As we drew closer to the wedding, I started to reflect on all the wonderful things that brought us to that point. As I did, I began feeling remorseful because I didn't formally propose to Tracey. Although it seemed fine with her at the time, I feared that in the future she might feel robbed of a precious memory.

I wanted to give Tracey a special wedding present that could only come from me. My pockets weren't very deep so I couldn't afford a lavish present. I decided to give her a gift that money couldn't buy, a song just for us. I sat down with my guitar and with little or no effort wrote a song entitled *From This Day On*. I decided not to tell Tracey about it, wanting her to hear it for the very first time during our vows.

The day had come and everything was perfect. Neither one of us had any butterflies, only a sense of calm. I remember seeing Tracey for the first time in her gown. Her Romanian heritage and style of dress made her appear a little old-fashioned. She looked beautiful but I was not surprised, she always did.

Our eyes stayed focused on each other's as she made her way down the aisle. The wedding march exemplified what we were feeling, causing our eyes to fill with happy tears. Tracey's dad tripped over the train of her dress, causing her to bust out with a belly laugh. It was more amusing than disruptive.

During the service, her fifteen-year-old sister, Lori, sang *You Needed Me*. Along with exchanging our vows, Tracey and I sang a duet. It was only fitting we sing to each other. That's how we met, how this whole thing started. We sang an old song entitled *True Love*.

I surprised Tracey when I turned to her and began singing the song I wrote especially for this day.

*From this day on, I'll give to you
A love that's strong, a love that's true.
We'll share our vows upon this day
And pledge to keep them in every way.
I love you so, and you love me too.*

*I'll be your strength if you weaken
I know that you too will be mine.
And as we ask for God's blessings
May he strengthen our hearts and our minds.*

*From this day on, we'll always be
Me for you and you for me.
So now we'll go, we've just begun.
We once were two, but now we're one.
I love you so, and you love me too.*

She loved the song, holding it dear to her heart from that moment on. My willingness to write it meant more to her than the song itself; another memory always worth remembering.

It was a very special day, but only a portion of the many blessings God had in store for us.

Chapter 9

Rocky Mountain High

I was the first to awake the next morning. I figured I would just lie in bed and stare at her until she stirred. I passed the time by watching the drool run down her chin and onto the pillow. She opened her eyes slowly, acknowledging that she felt me staring at her even in her sleep. Neither one of us felt the need to jump out of bed so we began to reflect on what just happened.

Our conversation wasn't only about the wedding. We went all the way back to the first time we met. So much had changed in both of our lives. One day, Tracey is calling me a jerk, the next day her husband. I reminded her from the moment I heard her sing, *Someone to Watch Over Me,* I knew I'd be the one who would.

She responded by saying, "Fine then, you can start by making me breakfast."

It was no secret that Tracey had no desire to cook. Maybe that's why she married me.

There was clearly a lot of changes going on in our lives, the natural by-product of a converted sinner. God was removing our "filthy rags" and clothing us with a "robe of righteousness" that only he could give. However, God didn't stop there. He not only became our "spiritual clothier," but he also took over the job of "Chief Contractor." As the Holy Spirit entered, he came with a "spiritual wrecking ball," wanting to do a complete renovation. God was creating a new heart where he would live, tearing down the *old shack* while building a *temple*. Only God could do the work, but we would still provide the "building permit" by yielding ourselves to him.

We were trying our best to be what God wanted us to be, but no one said it would be easy. In fact, the hardest part is not accepting Jesus as savior; it's living for him in a world filled with sin and temptation. Our nature is to sin, to give in to temptation, going all the way back to Adam and Eve.

However, we knew the Bible showed us we could resist temptation and sin through the power of the Holy Spirit living in us. We could live a sanctified life, holy and pleasing to God. Someone once said, *"You cannot stop a bird from flying over your head, but you do not have to let it build a nest on top of it."* The evil one will always try to tempt us, but God will always provide a way out so we don't give in. Jesus saves us from our sins but our salvation is in no way a license to continue in them.

I started working for a chain of jewelry stores in my local area. I started as a salesperson then moved to another store as assistant manager. Eventually, I ended up at a larger store in a mall as the assistant manager. Things were going great, two promotions in a short amount of time made me very excited!

I worked with mostly non-Christians. I was very zealous about my faith, believing that everyone needed to hear about Jesus; things were no different at my job. My manager told me I talked too much about God while I was working and should probably tone it down. I didn't know if I could do that, I cared about those people and felt they needed to hear the Word.

The vice president's son was still in college. He worked in our store during the holidays since he was grooming for the business. I liked him even though our relationship was a little confrontational at times. I was always trying to tell him about Jesus and he would find it offensive. Still, we got along well enough to have a good working relationship.

One night Tracey and I went on a double date with him and his girlfriend. We went out to eat and then decided to go bowling afterwards. His girlfriend was a gorgeous Italian girl. He was Jewish and she was very Catholic. I was always joking with him, telling him to leave the Gentile girls alone and go find himself a good Jewish girl. All night, I kept telling her to run while she could, which she eventually did. I wasn't getting close to converting him as much as making him mad.

One day my manager asked me to take a walk with him. We sat on a bench as he proceeded to tell me the young man's father, the vice president, wanted me to be let go. I asked why, but he said there was no reason given. I argued that it couldn't possibly be my work ethic, the company just promoted me twice in the last three months. He told me I was doing a good job, my performance at work had nothing to do with it. We had become good friends but there wasn't anything he could do about the decision. He started to cry while giving me a hug good-bye.

I was never told the real reason why I was let go. It would only be conjecture upon my part to say it had anything to do with my witnessing on the job. It wouldn't be fair for me to say it was the cause unless I had proof. I've always hoped that witnessing for Jesus was the reason for losing my job, I couldn't think of anything better to be guilty of.

I got a phone call from Pastor Charlie a couple days later. He called to say he was sorry to hear about me losing my job but also had something for me to consider. Our teens were going to the International Youth Conference in Colorado. They needed an adult to drive them out there and serve as a counselor. There was a man in our church who was supposed to go but something came up at work, causing him to cancel at the last minute. Charlie told me the conference was willing to pay my way since I just lost my job. Although there was a hitch, I had to leave the next day.

I called Tracey at her job and presented the situation to her, she was still upset about the job thing. She said she would think about it, asking when Charlie needed an answer. I told her it needed to be right away. She sighed quite heavily and asked if I thought I should be looking for a job instead. However, before I could answer she agreed that I should help out, believing I would find something when I got back.

The next day I took off with eighteen teenagers heading towards Colorado.

When we arrived, we were awestruck at just how breathtaking the mountains and scenery was. I knew this was going to be an emotional experience, especially spending time with a couple thousand teens in the midst of that splendor.

There were great messages throughout the week. The teens were very receptive to the Word resulting in hundreds of commitments. However, I wasn't experiencing the same kind of results when sharing with my group of kids. I was struggling during the afternoons as I tried to lead a devotional time with a collection of disinterested teenagers. We were using the same booklets as everyone else but for some reason my group wasn't participating or paying attention.

One day, my frustration got the best of me so I collected all the books from my group and threw them into the trashcan. I'm pretty sure the kids thought I was close to losing it. I decided that if they wouldn't listen then we'd just climb a mountain instead. Pretty rational don't you think?

After reaching the peak, we took a moment to soak in the magnificence of the view. It was awesome! We were so high you could see for miles and miles. The clouds were close enough that you could almost reach out and grab a handful. I could tell by their comments the teens found it mesmerizing. One said they felt closer to heaven while another marveled at how the "finger of God" had painted such a beautiful picture in nature.

Their attitudes were now completely different and they seemed eager to listen. They were glad we were there instead of doing the devotions back at camp. I knew I would be reprimanded for not following the lesson plan, but I really didn't care. I was determined to get inside their heads and hearts no matter what it took.

Someone put a mailbox on top of the mountain that had a Bible in it, probably why it was called *Bible Point*. I removed it from the mailbox and had my group sit down around me so I could read to them. I was not a trained or polished speaker, just an ordinary guy with a desire to tell people about Jesus. I was a new Christian myself and didn't know a lot about the Bible so I just opened it up and began reading.

I read about the *Good Shepherd* in John Chapter 10. As I did, I noticed the teens were listening more closely than before. After reading the whole passage, I began to explain what the story meant and how it could apply to them. They acted very interested in what I was saying and seemed to hang on every word. I was so encouraged my voice became more excited as I continued.

I never read or heard this story before so I obviously didn't prepare in any way. Nevertheless, I found myself having the ability to understand and discern how to communicate the meaning of every word. I no longer found myself sharing a devotional but *preaching* my very first sermon.

When I finished speaking, I had all the teens bow their heads and close their eyes. I shared that Jesus was the "gate" and the only passageway to Heaven. *"I am the gate; whoever enters through me will be saved."* (John 10: 9) I asked if any of them wanted to take a step of faith and enter through the gate to accept Jesus as their savior. My heart was blessed as a few responded with an uplifted hand signifying their desire to meet the Good Shepherd. These were the first converts I would lead to Jesus.

On this occasion, our time together ended with hugs and a greater feeling of togetherness. We started walking back down the mountain to the main camp. After a while, I separated from the group so I could walk alone and reflect on what had just taken place. Something strange and wonderful was happening on that mountain. I climbed up looking for a way to communicate to those teens; I walked down feeling a call upon my life to preach.

God was breaking my heart so I could preach to the broken hearted. He was giving me new eyes to see the lost and new lips to speak to them as well. I knew that as long as I filled my mouth with God's Word he would provide the ears to hear them. I could not wait to tell Tracey I found a new job in Colorado. It was obvious God had his hand in all of this, even me losing my job.

When I returned home, Tracey and I spent a lot of time talking about the decision to pursue a full-time ministry. It would take a whole lot of prayer and a lot more faith. Nevertheless, we would trust God to lead and provide.

Our first step in trusting God was not signing up for unemployment. I was eligible for it but we wanted to believe God for our finances. We didn't want to rely on anyone or anything else. It only took a short time for us to see God honoring our decision when Tracey got a promotion, increasing her salary by forty percent. It was exciting to see God confirming our decision to minister. We would work as though it was all up to us and pray as if it was all up to God.

Chapter 10

Worth the Wait

*O*ver the next months and years, God opened up many opportunities for ministry. I mailed out thousands of brochures trying to introduce myself to the churches. I trusted God for my bookings and he didn't disappoint.

At first, most of my engagements were concerts. I sang a lot of contemporary songs as well as my own original stuff so I got a lot of bookings centered more on the youth or from very progressive churches. My intentions were never to just entertain but to use the musical talent I had to open up opportunities to share the Gospel.

Many pastors and youth leaders liked the way I spoke to their teens. This led to many invitations to speak as the evangelist for teen camps and retreats. Over the years, I saw hundreds of young people draw closer to God. It was truly a privilege.

As time progressed, I had more and more pastors coming to hear me speak. I never spoke to the teens as if they were kids, but as adults. I never thought young people liked to see someone older than them trying to act like a teenager; they were too smart for that. I never watered down my messages, always approaching each service with a sense of urgency. Many pastors started contacting me to preach at their churches, feeling their adults were in need of hearing the same messages

In those days, churches were more committed to revival meetings. My schedule began to fill up with services all over the country. I wasn't raised in church yet many compared my preaching style to that of an old-time preacher. I didn't know exactly what that meant since I never heard any old-time preachers speak. It wasn't so much what I said, but more in the way I said it. I never pulled any punches, I always preached the Word with confidence. As a result, many people experienced "personal revival," not because of anything I had done, but because they sought God with their whole heart and found him.

Tracey would accompany me once in awhile, she sang while I did most of the speaking. She did enjoy going with me, it gave her the opportunity to pick on me in front of a lot of people. She felt a responsibility to keep me humble and in line. The audiences loved that she did and encouraged her even more.

Tracey would have traveled more, but she needed to dedicate most of her time to her career. Although I was staying busy, I didn't make much money as an evangelist. Tracey believed part of her ministry was to help with the finances, allowing me to go and preach the "Good News." She made the "bread" while I shared the "Bread of Life." We never wanted for what we truly needed, it was exciting to be partners in the Lord's work, whatever position we needed to take.

In all honesty, having my wife support us financially was a real *thorn in my flesh*. My male ego caused me to struggle with the situation, constantly tormented by the fact I was not the main provider. Nevertheless, Tracey was a godly woman, always reminding me that the souls saved and the lives touched were priceless. She would always say God was testing me to see if I was working for the right reasons. Nevertheless, it was still hard to swallow that the more faithful I was to preach the more money Tracey made.

Over the next four years, we saw much fruit in our ministry. However, we started to consider being fruitful in a different way, our conversations led to the subject of children. I never wanted kids up to that point. I might have been a little selfish or afraid to fail as a dad. I experienced many failures in life and did not want fatherhood to be another one. Tracey always wanted children but was willing to wait until I was ready.

One day, we visited some friends that just had a new baby boy. He was very cute but I had no interest in holding him. His mommy kept coercing me to try, but I refused. I used the excuse that I was afraid or I might drop him, but I really just wanted to be left alone. I knew what they were doing. Many people kept asking the question, "When are you going to have kids?" Now, they were turning up the pressure.

While Tracey was holding the baby, she walked toward me and placed him in my arms. She just let go and walked away laughing. I had to grab the kid so I wouldn't drop him. I started to yell and the baby reacted to my loud voice by crying. Right away, I started talking softly to him in some foreign language recognized by most as "baby talk."

As I stared into his little face, I felt something strange happening to me. I thought, "What a precious little boy." My heart started to soften as he wrapped his little fingers around mine. It was as though God was saying, "This is what I want for you."

On the way home, all I could talk about was that little baby. I told Tracey I thought it was time for us to have a child of our own, her eyes filled with tears as she agreed.

She knew God used that little boy to make me see what I was missing.

For the rest of the night we talked about what kind of parents we would be and what a big responsibility it was to be one. After much consideration, we agreed it was time to start calling ourselves parents. We began praying, asking God to bless us with a child. Tracey conceived right away, assuring us that it was God's timing.

Tracey worked right up to her delivery. She didn't experience much difficulty except for being treated with toxemia. She did what she was supposed to do to keep it under control, but her feet did swell until they hung over the sides of her shoes. She gained a little more weight than the doctors wanted, not seeming to cause her any problems. She could always diet and work out after the baby came.

The nine months seemed to fly by quickly, especially for me. Tracey carried the baby while all I had to carry was the suitcase. We went to all the Lamaze classes trying to learn all we could. I was so glad when those classes were over; my lungs were hurting from all those breathing exercises. Now it was just sit back and wait.

On the day after New Years, Tracey called me into the bathroom with the news that her water broke. I didn't want to be like all the fathers you hear about, running around like a chicken with its head cut off. I tried to be as helpful as I could while trying to hide my nervousness. Tracey on the other hand kept calm without needing much encouragement, she had mentally prepared for this moment a hundred times over.

We went to the hospital without breaking any speed limits, there was plenty of time; the baby wasn't coming anytime soon. Therefore, we waited, getting the usual updates every now and then. Tracey was progressing quite well until she started to feel ill. She was running a slight fever so they started watching the baby more closely. They went inside to attach a wire to the baby's head so they could monitor the oxygen level.

It was my job to go out and give reports to both our families, the longer it took the more I dreaded making the trip. I didn't feel like answering many questions but there were more and more each time I went out.

It was now almost twenty-four hours since Tracey's water broke. Up to this point, her pushing was to no avail. She was completely dilated, but her fever and the many hours of labor caused her to lose all strength. They started to get concerned about the baby because his oxygen level was low. The doctors said it was now time for Tracey to start pushing harder or they would need to perform a c-section. They said they would let her push just one more time.

Tracey began to cry while trying to push. She kept apologizing thinking that she was letting everyone down. All the nurses kept reassuring her she was doing great; it wasn't her fault. Tracey finally said, "I'm so sorry but I just can't push any more."

I felt so sorry for her. I was worried about the baby but she was my primary concern. I assured her the doctors knew what they were doing so she should continue to stay positive.

The doctor finally stepped back and said, "That's it, no more pushing. We need to get the baby out, get her prepped for surgery."

I tried to help her focus on the baby so she wouldn't think about what should have happened. I assured her that the c-section was the right thing to do, in a short while she would be holding her bundle of joy.

The doctor explained everything that would happen in the operating room and assured Tracey he would leave her with a scar that would allow her to wear a bikini. One of the nurses reassured her that the doctor was a master at leaving "invisible scars." Tracey just laughed, that was the last thing on her mind.

They started to wheel Tracey out of the room while telling me to say my good-byes. "Good-byes, I've got twenty-four hours invested in this." I shouted. "I'm not going anywhere."

Tracey was touched that I wanted to be by her side, although she did ask if I thought I might faint or get sick in the operating room, I've been known to get a little queasy at the sight of blood.

The nurse told me I could go into the operating room but there would be no one to care for me if I got sick or fainted. They would just push me into a corner until the surgery was over.

I accepted that and said quite emphatically, "Don't worry about me; you just take care of her."

I tried to talk with Tracey in the operating room as much as possible. She was in no pain and resigned herself to the events taking place. Occasionally, I would peek to watch the doctor as he made the incision. After looking, I told Tracey she was sure a "gutsy woman." She wasn't amused and I got a lot of dirty looks from the nurses, I was only trying to help take the edge off the situation.

I knew not to watch for very long, I wanted to be supportive but needed to make sure I didn't keel over. Normally, the blood from a small prick made me light headed. Watching them almost cut Tracey in half was a little more than I could take. By not focusing on myself, I was able to stay there and support her. I was learning you couldn't see the hurts of others and care for them as long as you only center on your own needs and problems.

The time had finally come. The doctor alerted us that our child was ready to make his debut into the world. He lifted him out of his mommy's belly announcing a beautiful baby boy. It was like looking right into Tracey's face, this little fellow was an absolute clone of his mommy, except for the gender obviously.

   I never saw a bigger smile on Tracey's face than I did at that moment, she was so proud. He was worth every moment of the struggle; he was *worth the wait*. It only took an instant for us to fall immediately in love with him. He was one second old, but it felt as though we had loved him forever. Only Jesus can fill a heart with that kind of instantaneous love.

   His name would be Joseph Paul, but we would refer to him as Joey. Joseph was Tracey's favorite Old Testament character, and Paul was my favorite from the New Testament.

   After I was sure Tracey was all right, I asked for her permission to watch them clean Joey up. Tracey realized how excited I was but knew I would never leave her side until she said it was okay.

   She said, "Oh, go ahead, I can't go anywhere. I'll just lay here while they suction me *out* and finish sewing me up."

   I'm sure she was a little jealous of me running around with my camera while she was still dealing with the operation. Hey, somebody had to get the pictures for posterity. The doctor was very nice, allowing me to take rolls of pictures as they cared for Joey. I knew how to get my way by staying out of the way.

   I could not believe this little person was my son. He was perfect in every way. I talked to him as I shot picture upon picture telling him I was going to be the best daddy in the world as well as his best friend. I promised I would teach him all about Jesus, how to talk with him and walk with him. The doctor just smiled as he listened to me. He was also a Christian and I'm sure pleased at what he heard. It didn't matter if Joey couldn't understand me. He would here those words every day for the rest of his life.

   Joey would play such a huge part in both of our lives, but in a very different way for Tracey. He was her special gift, coming directly from the heart of Jesus. What this "precious little lamb" would mean to Tracey is beyond human explanation.

Chapter 11

Breaking News

*E*very day was special with our new baby boy. Like most new parents, our world seemed to center around Joey and his needs, which was okay with us. I was determined to make sure I didn't miss anything as he was growing so I bought a nice camera and took pictures of him every day, never realizing how expensive it would end up being. No two people could have loved a child more than we loved Joey. Life was perfect.

A few months after Joey's first birthday, Tracey decided to start exercising. She was trying to lose the last few pounds of weight she gained during her pregnancy. After a while, she began to get into good shape, working out during her lunch hours not far from work. Now, her bodyweight was even less than before she got pregnant.

As time went on, Tracey began to feel some pain in her left thigh. She was convinced she had pulled a muscle; it seemed logical since she was exercising on a leg press machine. At first, she lowered the weight but saw no improvement. I told her just to work out on her upper body until the pain went away.

After cutting back, the pain persisted, increasing even without any stimulus. Tracey found herself limping more and more, causing her to go to the doctor although it took her a long time to make that decision. She was able to tolerate a lot of pain and felt too busy to bother running to the doctor. In other words she was stubborn.

Tracey never wanted to think anything could be wrong. It was her nature to always look for the positive and not think about the negative.

Since she was sure that her pain resulted from working out, she went to a sports medicine facility that had just opened. The doctor who examined her was Chief of Staff at the hospital. His diagnosis was that she probably had a damaged or pinched nerve based upon her age, activity, and the location of the pain. He proceeded to give Tracey the name of a neurologist to go see.

Unfortunately, during the examination this doctor failed to x-ray the leg to see if there was any visible damage, basing his diagnosis on experience and speculation rather than fact.

Tracey took her time calling for an appointment with the neurologist. It didn't seem that urgent since we were only talking about a *pinched nerve*. When she did finally call, she wasn't able to get in right away anyways which seemed okay at the time. She continued to limp more and more each day but it never stopped her from her daily activities.

During this time, Tracey and I decided to buy a larger house than the one we were living in. The home we were looking at was a bi-level home and much newer than the little house we owned. We felt it would be a much better place for Joey to grow up and go to school.

I'll never forget watching Tracey hobble around the backyard with the real estate agent. Her pain was so bad she started to have tears in her eyes almost all the time but she just tried to play it down.

It was now mid-September of 1986. There was a huge outdoor craft show not far from where we lived. It extended over a whole campground and people from all over came to shop. The theme was from the days of the early settlers and Tracey just had to go. I emphatically tried to talk her out of attending but she and her mom insisted on going. I reluctantly gave in although I was sure I would hate every moment.

It wasn't so much that I hated craft shows, which I did, but I couldn't stand to see Tracey in so much pain. I might have been the spiritual leader in our family but believe me it stopped there, Tracey did what she wanted, so off we went. Tracey's body seemed to buckle with every step she took making it harder and harder for her to negotiate the hills and stony paths. Still, somehow Tracey was able to enjoy herself despite the pain.

The fall was a busy time for me with revivals. I was preaching about two hours away in New Albany, Ohio. I decided to commute back and forth since it was not far away. I hated to be away from my family and it was not a problem for me to drive a couple of hours. When I got home late at night, I would always go into Joey's room and check on him. I would gently lift him and cradle him in my arms, careful not to disturb his sleep. I could sit staring at his precious little face for hours no matter how tired I was. He was my boy.

I always enjoyed my drive home because it meant I was going to see my family. However, on November 13, 1986 I came home to a note waiting for me instead of my family. The note said Joey was at my parents and Tracey was in the hospital, it mentioned something about her leg but was not specific. I jumped into the car and headed for the hospital wondering what could have possibly happened. I had no idea the *perfect life* as we knew it was about to change drastically.

Earlier that night, the phone rang prompting Tracey to jump from her chair to answer it before it awakened Joey. As she did, her leg collapsed beneath her causing her to fall to the floor in excruciating pain. She tried to stand but was unable; her leg would no longer support her weight. She began to pull herself across the floor to the phone to call for help, taking twenty minutes to crawl only fifteen feet. She called both her mother and my parents looking for whoever could get there the fastest to help her.

During her wait, Tracey grabbed the family Bible and just randomly opened to Philippians. As she began to read it aloud, she found herself almost yelling the words in the attempt to seemingly drown out the pain and retain consciousness. She did not know what was happening to her but did know was it was something very bad.

She found it even hard to pray through the pain now understanding what the Bible meant when it said, *"...the Spirit helps us in our weakness. We do not know what we ought to pray, but the Spirit himself intercedes for us with groans that words cannot express."* (Romans 8:26)

When everyone arrived, they were all so upset and confused Tracey ended up calling the paramedics herself. Upon first examination, the paramedics acted as though they thought Tracey might have been slightly exaggerating her symptoms. They were more patronizing than showing any sense of urgency. As they lifted her onto the stretcher, her leg began to swell, more than doubling its original size. Their eyes got as big as saucers as they finally recognized this was no exaggeration.

When I walked into the emergency room, I saw Tracey lying helplessly with her leg in traction. She began to cry as soon as she saw me, reaching for me as if to say, "Please help me, make this *yuck* go away."

She was trying to be so brave but I could see the scared look in her eyes. I promised her when we first met that I would always protect her but I didn't know how to at that moment. I tried to hold her but she stopped me before I could, the least little movement caused her unbearable pain. Even taking a breath brought a grimacing look to her face. The only thing I could do was hold her hand.

None of this made any sense. I was trying to grasp some semblance of understanding but there was nothing to hold on to. I could only ask, "What in the world happened?"

Tracey answered, "I don't know what happened. All I did was stand up and my leg just broke."

Tracey attempted to explain more of what took place but even she couldn't make sense of the whole situation. Her pain hindered her ability to think straight or even talk for that matter. All she knew was that an x-ray of her leg revealed that her femur bone had broken. That's why her leg was in traction, suspending it so it could keep the broken bone from moving or rubbing. But that still didn't tell us what happened.

The pain was overwhelming. At first, they wouldn't give her anything stronger than some Tylenol until the doctors came to some conclusion; it was obvious there was something more than just a pinched nerve. Tracey was normally mild tempered, but she started gritting her teeth and demanding something for the pain; she got it.

So what made it break? It was too early to get any conclusive answers from the emergency room doctors. One doctor said he thought he noticed something that looked like a tumor where the bone had broken. We discounted what he had to say, thinking there was no way that a tumor could be in her leg. We had just gone to the sports medicine doctor a few weeks before.

If only that first doctor would have x-rayed her leg, we might not have been in this situation.

The next morning, Dr. Mark Lesson came to talk to Tracey and me. The hospital contacted him to look at her case because he specialized in orthopedic oncology. Just that statement alone was sobering. Why was someone talking to us that dealt with tumors? How did we go from a pinched nerve to talking about cancer?

The doctor said he was quite sure there was a tumor in the bone after examining the x-rays. He believed it had been there some time, weakening the bone to the point of breaking. He said there were a couple of possibilities of what kind of tumor we were looking at. Nevertheless, he felt the need to let us know that cancer was the strongest candidate.

Dr. Leeson described the tumor as an *osteogenic sarcoma*, one that originates in the bone itself. He was hesitant to say for sure that it was this kind of cancer because it usually occurred in the early teens or adolescents; Tracey was twenty-eight. It was already a rare form of cancer but it would be even more extraordinary for Tracey to have it at her age. However, Dr. Leeson didn't want to speculate any further, he wanted to do a biopsy so he could make an accurate determination.

Tracey liked Dr. Leeson very much and she immediately put her trust in him. He spoke very directly, but also with compassion. Talking with her the way he did made Tracey feel he had a genuine interest in her. She made sure that he knew how much she already appreciated him. Tracey felt a need to reach out to the doctor by letting him know that a whole lot of people would be praying for him. God would help all of us to make the right decisions.

Chapter 12

When I am Weak, I am Strong

One of the most painful and disturbing things for Tracey was getting in and out of traction for the numerous scans and x-rays. She cringed every time they came to test her. Any movement at all caused the broken pieces of the bone to rub together increasing the ensuing pain.

One time an orderly came to take her down to x-ray, he was a very nice boy but slightly mentally challenged. While attempting to move her he rammed the corner of the bed into the casing of the door. Her leg began to swing back and forth causing Tracey to scream out at the top of her voice. The pain seemed just as intense as the initial break causing her to almost faint.

I started to jump across the bed in the attempt to get my hands around his neck. Tracey's leg wasn't going to be the only thing broken. Tracey pleaded, "No Denny! Please stop! I'm all right." Hearing her voice caused me to direct my attention back to her, keeping me from going any further.

The young man was very sorry but also very scared. Tracey was more concerned for the young man's feelings than the pain she felt. She assured him she was all right, no one was mad at him. She turned to me and said, "Isn't that right, Denny?" I agreed and then gave him a hug, apologizing for getting so upset with him. My witness and self-control paled in comparison to Tracey's self-discipline.

I befriended that young man and invited him to come and visit whenever he was on the floor. He stopped to see Tracey every day without fail, even on his days off. We looked forward to seeing him for he became very dear to us.

From that moment on, I turned into a control freak. One day I had a perfectly normal and healthy family. The next, pain and disease was growing far beyond our control. As a result, I grabbed tightly to any situation I could hold on to. I knew God was in control, but I couldn't just stand back and watch. I trusted Him for the big picture, but felt I needed to help with some of the small things. One thing was for sure. I would see that Tracey got the very best care from all the staff. I didn't want Tracey to have to experience any more hurt at least if it could be avoided.

Tracey was very nice to all the hospital staff. They all liked her and respected her as well. Many nurses were excited to care for her, bending over backwards to keep her comfortable. Some would come to see Tracey from other floors just to brighten up their own day. I thought Tracey would get the best care by cracking the whip. Tracey used a much stronger method, love and kindness.

During her stay in the hospital, Tracey counseled a few of the nurses for their spiritual as well as domestic needs. Their initial intentions were to help Tracey with her pain; instead, they found themselves pouring out their own hurts to her. God started to use Tracey to make a difference because of her willingness to look beyond herself and recognize the pain of others.

Tracey's family came to see her the morning of her surgery. Charlie, Brenda, and our friend Dwight also joined us. They all came to pray for Tracey and wish her well.

We told our doctor in advance that hundreds, maybe even thousands of people across the country were praying for Tracey's healing. We asked him to take just one more x-ray before the operation, just in case God saw fit to heal her. He agreed without any hesitation for he knew we were believers. The x-ray confirmed the tumor was still there. Tracey was at peace with the results.

It would have been wonderful if Tracey received a miraculous healing but that was not her primary request of God. Her first desire was for Jesus to get all the glory through the experience; that God would use her to draw others to him. Of course, Tracey prayed for healing, but she yielded herself to God's sovereignty, he had the final say. As Jesus faced death on the cross, he still prayed for his Father's will to be done and not his own. Tracey already decided that if she were more useful to God with one leg then she would *gladly bear the scars*.

We all prayed together. Everyone shared their love and promised to continue to pray as they waited. Before kissing her goodbye, I leaned over and told Tracey it was going to be awfully crowded in the operating room. She responded with a confused look. I explained that I was sure God would send a host of guardian angels to take care of his precious little girl. As they wheeled her away, I tried to keep smiling but my tears spoiled the facade.

Waiting is always an anxious time. I wasn't worried about Tracey spiritually, I knew she was trusting Jesus with everything. However, I was very worried about her physical condition after the operation.

This was a very invasive surgery and a major assault on her body. They were removing her whole leg without leaving even a stump. The expected pain would be tremendous and beyond my comprehension. I could only pray God would somehow ease her pain. I drew comfort from this verse as Jesus said, *"Come to me, all you who are weary and burdened, and I will give you rest. Take my yoke upon you and learn from me, for I am gentle and humble in heart, and you will find rest for your souls. For my yoke is easy and my burden is light."* (Matthew 11:28)

I don't remember the exact length of the surgery although I do know it was long enough to drain everyone as we waited. Praying seemed a much better choice than worrying but there were so many things to pray for I really didn't know where to start. I decided to put it all in God's hands.

The doctor finally appeared, looking quite exhausted. He told us the surgery went well and that Tracey would be in recovery for a long time. I thanked him for all he was doing and reassured him we had a lot of faith in him. He assured me that he did his best for Tracey, now it was time for her to heal.

As I waited for Tracey to get out of recovery, I began to visualize my first time seeing her as an amputee, I even started practicing what I would say and do. I knew my first reaction was crucial and something she would always keep in the back of her mind. In no way did I want her to think I looked or felt any differently towards her than before this surgery. It was so important to guard her feelings as well as take care of her physically. Leg or no leg she was my wife, nothing would change that. I wanted her to feel like a whole woman, she needed a husband that would treat her as such.

When they returned her to her room, I was told it was okay for me to see her. I remember sheepishly walking into the room saturated with the perspiration from worry. I was so anxious to say and do all the right things. As I reached for the door to push it open, the presence of the Holy Spirit assured me I was not walking in alone.

I was expecting to see a *wounded soldier* just returning from the front lines of a battlefield. Instead, I saw a beautiful angel sitting almost straight up in bed with the largest smile on her face. Tracey even had the nurse help comb her hair so she would look her best for me.

Tracey had enough morphine in her to force a bear into hibernation but her eyes were as big as saucers, wide-awake and very alert. This moment was so important to her. She was determined for me to know that she was still the same Tracey. Nothing about her was going to change except the way she walked. Her face just beamed with a look of childlike pride, as if to say, "I done good didn't I?" There was a sense of relief in my voice as I asked, "Am I in the wrong room? I don't see anyone sick in here. You look too pretty to have just had an operation."

Tracey responded, "There's no one sick in this room, not anymore."

As I approached the bed, I continued to stare at her face, careful not to drop my eyes where her leg was missing. I wanted to make sure Tracey realized I loved her for who she still was, not for what she looked like. We needed to dwell on what we still had, not on what was lost. As I reached down to hug her I whispered in her ear, "Are you all right baby girl?"

Tracey began to cry as she responded, "I'm all right. Just hold me and never let go."

I replied emphatically, "I won't. I promise."

She had both her arms around my neck, squeezing so hard it almost choked me. Tracey's hold never lessened as we continued to embrace one another, staying in that position until all her tears were gone. She found sanctuary in my arms as she felt the love of Jesus through my human touch. God was using me to be Tracey's *power adapter*, gaining strength from him through exposing her weaknesses to me.

Her body felt so small and fragile, I felt as though I might break her if I held her too tightly. She lost a lot of weight and with the leg gone weighed only eighty-eight pounds. Nevertheless, God was preparing this *broken vessel* for his purpose and use. Through her weakness, God would display his strength. In her darkness, God would shine his light.

Like the Apostle Paul, Tracey had asked God to remove the "thorn in the flesh," hers was cancer. We both believed God's response was the same, *"My grace is sufficient for you, for my power is made perfect in weakness."* (2 Corinthians 12: 9) Instead of hiding her handicap, Tracey would learn to boast about it. *"For when I am weak, then I am strong."* (2 Corinthians 12:10)

After finally releasing her grip from my neck, Tracey pulled the blanket down and showed me her bandaged stump. She said, "Well, I did it Denny, here's what's left of me." I immediately put my hand gently on top of the bandages to assure her she didn't repulse me in any way. I called it her "little leggy" which would stick from that moment on.

I reminded her, "What happens to one of us, happens to all. We share in the good times and in the bad."

Although there is a difference between physical and emotional pain, it's still pain. I asked Tracey just how bad the pain was. She said the drugs were working for the most part but refused to allow it to consume her. *Her most powerful painkiller was Joey.* Every time she began to hurt, she just focused on her baby boy instead of her pain. She missed holding him and knew it would be some time before she was healed enough to play with him. Through a mental calendar, Tracey had already started counting the days until she was able to go home and be with her Joey.

Tracey's mom bought her a statue of a large hand holding a small girl. Tracey envisioned herself to be that little girl, snuggled safe in the hand of her Savior. During her lonely times in the hospital, she would gaze at the statue while being comforted by its significance. It became one of her most prized possessions, understandably so.

We were not so naïve to believe any of this was going to be easy. Every day presented some kind of new challenge, obstacle, or disappointment. We knew there was far more truth in the words of the song, *Because He Lives*, than anything the well-meaning counselor had shared with me. It was obvious to us our relationship would be fine as long as we trusted God for our future. Jesus was the invisible, yet ever-present adhesive that would hold our family together; nothing could separate us from his love.

Tracey's relationship with the Lord was growing deeper because of what she was going through. Having to face cancer, amputation, and the possibility of death produced more of a dependence on God than ever before. Although the cancer would slow Tracey down physically, her spiritual walk accelerated. Tracey's desire was to be more like Jesus. The Bible says, *"...to offer your bodies as living sacrifices, holy and pleasing to God..."* (Romans 12:1)

The deeper you go, the broader you grow. It might sound like a cliché, but the more you trust God for your ministry the more he can trust you with it. Tracey's faith was no longer under a microscope but a magnifying glass. Friends and family who once questioned the size of Tracey's faith now found themselves blinded by its enormity.

Tracey had a tremendous love for all her immediate and extended family. Up to this point, she felt her family tolerated her witness more than accepted it. She had a deep burden for all of them to know Jesus and realize heaven; she prayed for them faithfully.

During this hospital stay, Tracey shared with me that she believed God was answering her prayers by allowing this cancer to happen in her life. She believed the only way her family members would ever know Jesus was if they saw him bigger than ever before. To this point, her seemingly perfect life had no real impact on leading any of them to Jesus. Maybe now they would see the light in this dark time.

Tracey lost her leg but gained a new boldness. She stated confidently, "If anyone comes to see me, they're going to hear about Jesus! My hospital room is my pulpit."

This new Tracey excited the "soul winner" in me. Now, instead of admonishing me for being too bold, Tracey was joining me.

God was lifting Tracey onto a pedestal to be a witness to the lost and a challenge to the saints. Most visitors entered her room looking for a helpless victim of a handicap, but instead found a dynamo for Jesus. *"Humble yourselves before the Lord, and He will lift you up."* (James 4:10)

After awhile, Tracey started to feel well enough to accept visitors. Most all of them came to encourage Tracey and some to show their sympathy. More times than not, the visitors went away with more encouragement from Tracey. She made it so hard for anyone to feel sorry for her. In fact, if you still felt sorry for her after visiting her you really didn't see her. She inspired most with her strong faith and convicted some because of their lack of it.

Tracey stood true to her word about sharing Jesus. She didn't necessarily preach to anyone, but never failed to give God the glory for carrying her through. Tracey's family loved her very much. They thought they knew her well, but they would now discover even more about her.

One particular visit that stands out in my mind is when her Uncle Ronnie came to visit her in the hospital. They thought the world of each other. Tracey looked up to her Uncle Ronnie as a leader in the family. She always thought getting him to church would cause the rest of them to follow. Ronnie always felt a gentle nudging from Tracey to go to church, acknowledging that Tracey always said, "All I ever wanted was for all of us to go to heaven."

Before leaving the hospital Uncle Ronnie promised, "Honey, if there is anything in this world I can do for you, all you have to do is tell me and I will do it."

That's the night Tracey's gentle push turned to shove. Tracey's reply to him was, "I'm going to speak at my church the first Sunday I'm out of here. I would love for all my family to be there."

Ronnie answered sadly, "Honey, that's a beautiful request, but please don't be disappointed if it doesn't happen."

With a sad but firm voice, Tracey replied, "I will be."

Tracey would never be one to talk back to an elder family member but her burden for them was greater than ever. She didn't care if it seemed manipulative; she was on a mission. Tracey thought if she could endure what she was going through, they could surely tolerate going to church. Because of their deep love for Tracey and the earnestness of her request, the majority of her family decided to attend church to hear her speak.

Chapter 13

Time to Witness

The hospital stay was over, time to bring mommy home. Joey was excited for the big day but not as much as Tracey. She was looking forward to sleeping in her own bed where it was much quieter, at least when Joey was asleep. The people at the hospital treated her well but Joey and I decided that we would pamper her even more. She was still in a lot of pain so we tried to make her as comfortable as possible. A hug from Joey always seemed to make the pain a little more tolerable.

Pastor Charlie told Tracey she could have the whole service to share her testimony the first Sunday after breaking out of the hospital. She could not wait to speak to all her friends and loved ones. Although it may be contrary to most logical thinking, she wanted to debut the "new and improved" Tracey.

The sanctuary filled up with people anxious to hear Tracey speak. Before she spoke, we sang the song *What a Difference You Made in My Life*. We wanted everyone to understand that knowing Jesus allowed us to face our trying times in a way different from the world. Skeptics have asked,

"Don't you think you could have gone through this without Jesus?"

Tracey's answer would be, "I really don't know, I would never want to try."

Almost every day millions of people go through horrific situations without knowing Jesus. Their road is much harder and a whole lot lonelier.

Tracey began to share, "Before I speak, I want to sing a song for you, *No One Ever Cared for Me Like* Jesus. I've sung it many times and it becomes more and more real every time I sing it. I have to share with you, at this moment it's more real to me than ever before." Tracey began to sing while the congregation commenced to cry.

After singing, Tracey continued to speak. "I thought for a long time about what I was going to say this morning. You can ask all the people I work with, I always try to plan ahead by writing things down. However, I didn't write a lot down this morning. I have a few notes here and few things there. What I want to tell you this morning is not prepared, its coming straight from the heart of Jesus; straight from my heart to yours."

Before going any farther, Tracey asked everyone to sing the chorus *God is So Good* with her. They formed a beautiful choir as they sang it acappella. They sang the verses *God is So Good, I Love Him So, and He Answers Prayer.*

Tracey responded with tears in her eyes, "Thank you for singing that for me. You've just ministered to me."

"Many people would come here today and say, 'Look at that girl up there. She just lost her leg only a few weeks ago. Why would she be up there singing, "God is so good," she must be crazy!'

"Well let me tell you something, I've never been happier than I am right now. I may only have one leg, but it's planted firmly on the "solid rock" of Jesus Christ. As long as I've got even one leg on that *Rock*, I'll be stronger than anyone you might meet on the street who doesn't know my Jesus.

"I want to minister to you but I first want to thank you for ministering to me. When I look out there, I see so many people. Almost my entire family is sitting in the first two rows of this church. I want to personally thank you from the bottom of my heart for your support and for your love. You spent many days and nights in that hospital for over a month. You loved me through writing me notes. This morning my Aunt Sherry gave me this whole book where everyday she wrote another promise of Jesus for me. I want to thank each and every one of you for everything. You've been so special to me ever since I've been a little girl. You'll never know how much you've meant to me.

"Also, in the back there's a bunch of people I've worked with for over ten years from the *Malone Advertising Agency*. They're like family. You wouldn't believe the encouragement I've been getting from them. Everyday my mailbox was filled with twenty or thirty cards saying, 'Tracey I'm praying for you, I'm pulling for you, and I know you're going to be back here soon.' It means so much.

"I've learned so much. I've learned how to appreciate people through all of this; in the same way you've appreciated me. The cards, the notes, the letters from fellow workers and from my clients, there was no way that Jesus wasn't present when there was that much love flowing around.

"Then of course, there's my church family. I appreciate you so much. Thank you for ministering to me, thank you for praying for me. I bet your phone lines were tied up from praying for Tracey on the prayer hot line. Everyday it was something new and everyday you prayed me through. I thank you for that very much.

"There are so many people to thank. Someone here did special things for me while I was in the hospital. Her name is Susie Finny, a dietician at City Hospital. She has her uniform on so she must have snuck out to be here this morning. Jesus talked about giving *cups of cold water* to people, those little things that mean so much. Everyday at two o' clock Susie made sure I received a milkshake. I was the only patient in the whole hospital that received a milk shake at that precise time.

"I've learned so much about caring for people. I thought I knew how to before but I've learned so much more. The way you've cared for me has taught me the way to care for others, so I thank Jesus for this experience. We go through life so fast sometimes, just kind of zooming through. We do things so quickly we just never realize those special moments. I thank everyone here for all of those special moments I have of each one of you. I will always carry them with me as an encouragement.

"I guess what I'm supposed to do is to tell you a little bit about what happened to me. You know me. I don't like to talk about the bad news; I only like to talk about the good parts. But I think it is only through those bad moments that you can recognize how wonderful the good moments are."

Tracey went on to share the way her leg broke and the events that happened throughout her hospital stay.

She continued, "Pretty soon you're going to see me with a leg because I'm already being fitted for my new one. I keep telling Joey, 'Don't worry its coming back.' Joey came to get me in the hospital and said 'Mommy where'd your leg go?' I said, 'It's broken but we're getting a new one.' It's so precious when children are two years old. They just say okay; worrying is for the adults.

"After I got out of the hospital, I went to the doctor for a check up. A lady came up to me and said, 'You're so pretty.' She didn't notice I was missing my leg. Now, it's not too often someone comes over to you and just tells you how pretty you are. It was as though God planted a little angel to come and sit down beside me just to make me feel good. It made me realize that it doesn't matter what you see on the outside. I have to learn more of that. Sometimes we are so impressed by what's on the outside of people we don't see what's going on inside.

"There are so many things we have to be thankful for, especially during this Christmas season. We rush through each day doing all the things we think are important and they're usually not. They turn out to be what are urgent for that moment. They have to be done right now whether they matter or not; and they usually don't matter.

"I spent many afternoons doing unimportant things like shopping instead of being at the hospital. I could have been like Susie, giving someone a milkshake and asking them how they're doing. It would have been so much better to add a smile to someone's face instead of another gift in my shopping bag. There's no limit to what one can do with just an encouraging word that comes from a heart filled with love; the love that Jesus puts inside.

"I think some people expected me to say I couldn't do this, but Jesus knew I could. He knew I was going to make it. He knew everything was going to be all right. I prayed that God would give me a feeling of assurance and hold my hand. I know people might say God can't do that, but he did, and I felt it. I felt the warmth of his hand in mine as he told me that I could do anything.

"There's a saying that says, 'Lord give me the guidance to know when to hold on and when to let go and the grace to make the right decision with dignity'.

"I felt like I was making the right decision. I felt as though I was doing what he wanted me to do. In this decision, I knew only good things would happen. I can assure you since my operation only good things have happened. I've gotten to know my family better. I look at my precious little boy and realize how special he really is. Children are so beautiful and families are so beautiful. Even the people that get on your nerves at work are still wonderful people. You have to look for the positive things in people and I praise God that I'm going to look for those things even more.

"After my surgery, I went down for therapy and learned to walk with crutches. I worked really hard because I wanted to get out of there. The therapist told me I was learning faster than anyone he had worked with before. I told him it was because I really wanted to go home. He told me I was different from most of the people he saw and wanted to know why. Most people were basket cases after losing a leg.

"I said, 'Well, maybe you've never met anyone who knows Jesus as closely as I do. He's been with me through the whole thing and I count it a privilege for Jesus to be as real to me as he is. He was real before, but never as real as he is now. We have friendly conversations. Now I've prayed, but I prayed the regular prayers, like help people get well and help me through this or that. But we talk to each other all the time now and it feels wonderful.'

"After hearing this, his first response was, 'Oh I'm sorry, I swore yesterday.' I said, 'No, no, no, don't worry about it. That's not what's important. The most important thing is that you know that the Jesus I've found, you can find too. He's not exclusively my Jesus.'

"You who are here today might think I can do this but you couldn't. You're no different than I am. In fact, there are a lot of you who are much stronger than I am. It's not me, but the Jesus in me that makes these things possible.

"I do want to share something with you. All of you mean so much to me and you mean so much to Jesus. You're special even though you might not feel that way right now. You may feel there are some things you don't like about yourself. I have a good reason not to like some things about myself. I don't look *normal* when I look in the mirror but I don't see myself as *abnormal*. I see myself how Jesus sees me, completely whole again.

"Handicapped; I don't feel handicapped. When you're handicapped there are a lot of things you can't do, they say. The Bible tells me that through Christ I can do all things. There's nothing I can't do through him as he empowers me. I might not be walking with my own leg, but I guarantee *I'll be walking. 'I can do everything through Him who gives me strength.'* (Philippians 4:13)

"Another thing I'll be doing is being a better person to each one of you. I want to be a better friend; a better daughter, a better niece, cousin, grandchild, and I want to be a better church member here at this church. But most of all I want to be better for my Jesus, for he deserves it. He's always there for me and I hope that now I will be there for him."

Tracey's courage and deep faith inspired her whole family. God opened their eyes to see beyond the human hurt to recognize the spiritual healing. Many began to attend our church and over the next several years, at least twenty-eight members of her family had come to know Jesus as savior. Even recently, Ronnie's son, Rob, has been ordained an elder in the Free Methodist Church. Each family member was special to Tracey. She showed no favoritism. However, she did have a favorite story.

Her 88-year-old grandfather, affectionately called *Papa Loo*, was in the hospital. Pastor Charlie went to visit him and asked if he had ever asked Jesus to be his personal savior. Not knowing necessarily how to answer, grandpa said, "Well, I know I'm a good man. I've never done anything wrong or ever hurt anybody."

Again, Pastor Charlie asked the same question. Grandpa answered Charlie's question with a question of his own. "If God is so good, then why did He let this happen to Tracey of all people? She's one of the nicest people I know; no one's better. Of anyone I know she doesn't deserve it."

Charlie went on to explain that bad things do still happen to good people. He told grandpa that Tracey wasn't sad, but happy. Happy because all she ever wanted was for all of her family to go to heaven with her and now so many are.

"Then I want to go too," replied Grandpa.

Charlie prayed with Grandpa as he accepted Jesus right there in the hospital.

Tracey's grandpa was far more important to her than her leg. Losing her leg was a small price to pay if it helped *Papa Loo* find Jesus.

Chapter 14

Niagara Falls

It was almost Christmas and Tracey felt badly that she didn't get to go shopping for her family, especially for Joey. Her mom was more than willing to do the shopping for her but Tracey insisted we go to the mall. She wanted to be more involved than just making a list. Anyways, cabin fever had set in and she was going stir crazy just sitting in the house, even if it was doctor's orders.

I was reluctant to go trying desperately to talk her out of it. I was in my protective mode, not wanting her to incur any physical setbacks. In addition, I was worried she might be humiliated if people stared or pointed at her, I was sure they would. A busy mall at Christmas was not my idea of a good choice to be in public for the first time as an amputee.

I'm sure you've already guessed who won the argument so off to the mall we went. At first, Tracey was a little tentative with her crutches, but it didn't take long before she was zipping along from store to store. I stayed as close as possible just in case she slipped.

Hundreds of stitches were holding her entire left hip together and I wanted to make sure they stayed there.

Everyday, I would clean the stitches, then wrap the stump tightly with an ace bandage; something I really wasn't called to do, but needed to do. She might not have been that fragile nonetheless I cared for her as if she was.

Tracey was dressed in a baggy sweatshirt and sweatpants for comfort. We rolled up the left pant leg all the way to the hip secured with a large safety pin. It was nearly impossible for someone not to notice her as she made her way down the mall. As I imagined, everyone almost tripped over themselves as they stopped to gawk at her.

At first, I tried to ignore their insensitivity by not making eye contact with them. I noticed Tracey was doing the same by walking with her eyes fixed only a few feet in front of her. I could only take so much so I started staring people down with contemptuous eyes. Most would immediately look away when they saw me staring back at them.

As we approached a small group of people, they started whispering among themselves while pointing at Tracey. "What are you looking at?" I shouted in anger. My big voice echoed throughout the mall, drawing even more attention that was unwelcome. They all quickly turned and began to walk away.

Tracey quit walking and shouted at me, "Stop it! Just stop it!" I answered back. "I won't stop it! I'm sick and tired of these people gawking at you! Do you really expect me to just stand back and let them make a spectacle of you without saying anything? I'm here to protect you."

Tracey bit back saying, "Your yelling at them hurts me more than them staring at me. If they don't bother me, then why should they bother you? You promised only to help me when I asked for it and I'm not asking! I know I'm going to be stared at the rest of my life and I'll have to accept it. I won't accept being embarrassed by you."

I apologized, sharing that my intentions were to never hurt or embarrass her. I promised never to yell at anyone again, although when Tracey wasn't looking I still gave them dirty looks.

As we were leaving the mall, a little girl about four years old stopped and pointed at Tracey. She yelled out "Look mommy, that lady only has one leg!" Her mother was mortified, pleading for Tracey's forgiveness while grabbing the little girl's hand to whisk her away.

Tracey began to laugh and said, "Oh, don't worry about it, she's just being honest. She's right, that's what I am, a one-legged lady."

The woman laughed and thanked Tracey for understanding.

I saw in Tracey what Jesus meant when he said, *"Father forgive them, for they do not know what they are doing."* (Luke 23:34) Jesus was being shamed and crucified yet he cared more for those who persecuted him than he did himself. Likewise, Tracey easily forgave people for their ignorance and put their feelings above her own. She thought people might not do or say certain things if they understood just how much it hurt others; ultimately, bringing shame upon themselves.

It was obvious Tracey was ready to face the world as an amputee, somehow she didn't see herself the way others saw her. Jesus had given her so much grace it was overflowing onto others.

Christmas was a joyous time. Joey got all the presents he could ever want and Tracey got what she wanted, being at home with her family. I cancelled all the meetings and concerts I had booked during that time, but kept the one for New Years. I was to be the song leader for a large teen gathering in Niagara Falls.

I could tell by the way Tracey was acting that she had an interest in going with me. Before, I would usually go by myself while she worked or stayed at home with Joey. When I asked if she wanted to go with me she accepted without any hesitation. I told her the only stipulation was that the doctor had to okay the trip. Tracey agreed, so we made an appointment to have her checked out for traveling.

When we saw the doctor it was apparent he was as equally concerned for Tracey's mental state as he was for her physical condition. He thought her going with me would be good for her psychologically, but made her promise she would take it easy.

We arranged for my family to watch Joey while we were gone, they were always helpful in taking care of him. Tracey's Uncle Ronnie offered us his big Cadillac when he heard she was going. It offered a lot more room than our vehicle, providing more comfort for Tracey.

It was only a four-hour trip but grueling for a girl who just had her leg removed. Tracey was uncomfortable yet never complained. She was so excited to do anything that seemed close to normal. She was determined not to allow pain or discomfort to keep her from living life to the fullest.

She sat very still during the whole trip frequently asking, "Are we there yet?" She looked like a little girl who couldn't wait to get out of the car after a long vacation trip.

Upon arriving, we sat in the car for a while before going in. I asked, "Are you ready for this?" Tracey answered with a large sigh, "I've always got to be ready."

We both knew just how discriminating a teenager could be, multiply that times five hundred. I wasn't worried about Tracey especially because of the way she handled herself with the discourteous shoppers. I was just praying the teens would be kind to her when they first saw her.

We walked into the convention center spying what seemed to be an army of busy bees going in all directions. I have never seen so much energy concentrated into one place. The older guys were chasing the girls, while the younger guys were running from them. Many gals were checking out the cute boys as the guys put together their top ten lists of babes. The popularity contests had already started amongst the young ladies and the fellows were vying for who was most macho, just typical teen stuff.

Suddenly, a young girl with only one leg came zipping by on crutches. Her eyes met Tracey's and instantly a bond formed between them. She stood out in the crowd, not because of her amputation, but because of her high energy and outgoing personality.

Tracey looked at me with tearful eyes and said, "I'm supposed to be here." I responded, "Yea, probably more than we'll ever know."

When Tracey finally tracked her down, we found out the young girl was from Michigan. More importantly, she told us she had the same cancer as Tracey. She had her surgery sometime earlier and had already undergone some chemotherapy treatments. She had a prosthesis with her, but got around a lot faster on crutches.

She had no inhibitions because of the way she looked. In fact, she seemed to be one of the most popular teens there. It was so obvious Jesus was doing a great work in this beautiful girl's life. The two of them agreed to keep in touch, coveting to pray for one another.

It was so encouraging that this young girl welcomed Tracey to that event. When Tracey first found out she herself had cancer, she started grasping on to the things that gave her hope and purpose for her life. *Knowing there were more people like her gave her purpose; knowing they were alive gave her hope.*

Tracey was unaware but I talked to the director of the convention, asking him if we could find some time for Tracey to speak to the teens. We both agreed her testimony could make a great impact on their lives. I wanted to make sure it was possible before springing it on Tracey. When I approached her with the idea, she was more than willing and began to prepare what she might say, although I knew it would be mostly from her heart. I took some of her music along so she also could also sing.

When it came time for Tracey to speak, we put a stool in the middle of the stage for her to sit and talk. After her introduction, she slowly made her way up a steep set of stairs to the platform. As she shyly made her way across the stage, everyone stood to greet her with a standing ovation. I was standing off to the side and out of sight. I was so proud of the way she handled herself through all of this. I didn't know whether to smile or cry, so I chose to cry. There was such a big person inside of that little body. My heart flowed with the same feelings a parent has when watching their child dance at their first recital or hit that first home run. I remember whispering to myself, "Help her Jesus."

Tracey was overwhelmed by the reception she received from this group of young people. She expected them to be one of the toughest crowds she had ever faced. Instead, they turned out to be one of the warmest.

She was yet to make eye contact with the audience. She felt a little nervous and a bit shy as she fumbled with her crutches, making sure they were never out of her reach. When they put the microphone in her hands, it was like offering a baby a pacifier or security blanket. Give a singer a microphone and they will feel at home anywhere.

Tracey finally looked into the eyes of her audience and greeted them. "Thank you so much. You don't know how much that means to me." She took a deep breath and regained her composure. She felt it a privilege to be sitting in front of those young people as well as a big responsibility. They were the most attentive, wide-eyed group she had ever seen, all on the edge of their seats just waiting to hear what she had to say.

Tracey shared a little of what had happened to her but focused more on the decisions she made preparing her for it. She began to tell her story.

"When I was about your age I made the most important decision of my life, to accept Jesus as my personal savior. I would not be sitting in front of you today if I had not made the right choices as a teenager.

"In my senior year, my classmates voted me the most popular girl in class as well as homecoming queen, and I was not a "secret agent Christian." I never had to hide that I was a Christian to be popular, in fact being a Christian helped make me popular.

"People liked me because I treated them the way Jesus taught me to. If they didn't like me or made fun of me Jesus gave me the security not to let it bother me. It's that same security that allows me to sit in front of you with one leg without feeling embarrassed or less than whole. *I may only have one leg, but that leg is planted firmly on a "Solid Rock," the solid rock of Jesus.*

"Some call people like me a handicap because I've lost my leg to cancer. Yes, I have a leg missing, but I'm still whole, *whole inside.* I notice many of you are crying because you maybe feel sorry for me, but please don't, I'm really all right.

"You are here tonight and have all your parts. The only thing missing is Jesus, but that makes you more handicapped than me. My handicap is just more of an inconvenience. It might keep me from getting into certain places but your handicap, not knowing Jesus, will keep you from getting into Heaven. You have all your limbs but you're not whole. There's an empty hole in your life that only Jesus can fill. You'll try to fill that void with sex or popularity, money or maybe even drugs, but only Jesus can satisfy the empty space in your soul, because that's how God designed you."

Tracey sang the song *No One Ever Cared for Me Like Jesus.* She elaborated more on how young people put too much emphasis on their outward appearance while neglecting what they looked like on the inside. She challenged them not to allow themselves to be judged by their looks or what designers name appeared on the clothes they wore. She reminded them that they looked exactly the way God wanted them to look. Not accepting what you look like is the same as telling God to his face, "You made a mistake when you made me."

His answer would be, "You're wrong, for I made you in my image."

When Tracey finished speaking, she went down onto the floor where a crowd of girls surrounded her, all jockeying for position so they could talk to her.

Most of their eyes were bloodshot from crying. Two girls particularly caught Tracey's attention. Both of them were sobbing uncontrollably so Tracey tried to comfort them.

"Don't cry I'm really all right."

The girls said, "We're not crying for you, we're crying for ourselves. We want to be whole, just like you."

We prayed that those teenagers would now look at themselves differently when they gazed into a mirror. Tracey challenged each teen to look beneath their clothes and makeup and beyond the figure of their body, seeing all the way to their heart. If it is broken, ask Jesus to mend it. If it is empty, invite Jesus to come in.

Tracey was realistic enough to realize most people looked at her amputation as something ugly and abnormal. If they looked beyond the handicap, they were able to see the real beauty of the whole person she really was. Before her cancer, people would glance at her and see a pretty girl. Now, those same people would stare at her and see Jesus.

The world focuses so much on outward beauty that it becomes a deterrent for most people to work on the inside. Society honors people for far less than they work for or deserve. The world admires a beautiful woman for having a great set of legs, while ignoring the blackness of her heart.

The same world looked beyond Tracey's leg and admired the fullness of her life.

We stayed in touch with the young teen that had lost her leg. Some time after the convention, we heard her cancer had resurfaced. We made a special trip to visit see her with the intentions of trying to encourage her family. Not long after our visit, we received news that this precious young girl had lost her battle with cancer.

Tracey was very disturbed by the news. Her hope for herself had taken a large blow as the reality of death exposed itself through this young girl.

Chapter 15

Fear Is Not an Option

The trip to Niagara Falls was a tremendous uplift to Tracey but not without consequence, it was just too early for her to be so active. Some of the stitches had broken, leaving a gaping hole in her stump. Therefore, it was back to the hospital for some corrective surgery, the one place we did not want to go.

By this time, the bills for the surgery and hospital stay started coming in the mail. It was unbelievable how expensive everything was. We had good insurance, but even the incidentals and the things not covered were starting to add up into the thousands of dollars. Although it was of some concern, we were determined not to let money, or the lack of it, become primary.

We trusted God completely with our finances. We tried to be faithful givers, not out of any compulsion but because it just felt good. We wanted to give back a portion of what God gave us, believing God would provide a way for us to pay our hospital bills and home expenses. How he did was far beyond what we would have been comfortable to ask for.

I shared earlier we now lived in a bi-level home, not conducive for a handicapped person. The garage was on the lower level so when we came home we had to climb two flights of steps to reach the main floor. Although Tracey was getting comfortable with the crutches, she was still anxious about negotiating all those steps.

When the news of Tracey's operation had spread, some of the conversations included the problem of the steps. Right away, God started looking for a remedy for our predicament. He spoke to an anonymous donor who provided us with not one, but two lifts; one for each set of stairs totaling over five thousand dollars.

That donor has never come forward but I am sure God has blessed them many times over for their kindness and generosity. It's my hope that I can somehow show my expression of thanks through this book.

God does wonderful things through his most faithful servants. We never asked for those lifts but God knew we would need them. He also knew the right person to speak to about them. It's amazing to see what happens when man's obedience works in conjunction with God's faithfulness. God was supplying our needs through others he had already provided for. *He was not through.*

Pastor Charlie sent out a letter across the denomination containing an explanation of our situation and our request for prayer. The response was beyond anything we could have ever predicted. Every day our mailbox overflowed with cards and letters full of encouraging words and promises to pray for us. People we didn't even know were coveting to lift us up in prayer and we sure felt it.

However, there were more than just promises for prayer inside those cards. God's people were joining our struggle and investing in our lives through monetary gifts as well. Almost every card contained a love offering to help defray any expenses we might incur. There were some individual gifts but most of the cards came from churches that took up special love offerings. No matter how large or small we appreciated each gift.

The expressions of love and concern were overwhelming to both Tracey and me. Many of the letters came from churches I had ministered in, touching me the most. Along with their gifts were stirring words of how much they appreciated my work while ministering in their churches. They expressed that they received help in the special meetings and now it was their turn to help us.

Many of the offerings sent by some churches actually exceeded the amount of payment I received while preaching there. I must admit, sometimes I felt disappointed by the small amount of pay I earned when preaching, but never enough to want to stop. I have never been a lover of money but one does have to survive. I would not have been able to continue in the ministry if Tracey didn't work fulltime. There's a big difference between needing money and wanting it. You don't have to hate it, but it is unhealthy to love it. *"Whoever loves money never has money enough; whoever loves wealth is never satisfied with his income."* (Ecclesiastes 5:10)

It seemed as though God through his omnipotent wisdom held back part of my earnings. It was God's way of saving for a "rainy day" when he knew I wouldn't. When the "storms of life" came pouring down on us God took what he held in deposit and added interest far beyond what any earthly bank could ever give. In one day alone, we received enough money to pay for a whole year of mortgage payments. I'm not sure exactly how much we received but I do know it was more than enough to pay every bill we had and then some. I felt it was God's way of saying to us, "You focus on your family, and I'll handle the finances."

Tracey's artificial leg, more commonly known as a prosthesis, was finished and ready to pick up. She had her fitting after she got out of the hospital but had to wait for her incisions to heal before trying to use it. It was amazing to us how skilled people can take different materials and design them to help an amputee function so close to normal.

Tracey was so excited when they brought the leg to her for the first time. They did an outstanding job, making it look exactly like her other leg. I examined it closely and then said to Dan Shamp the owner, "So this costs eight thousand dollars, huh? For that much money it *better grow hair!*" Somehow, I think he might have heard that one before. It didn't matter how much it cost, as long as it would help Tracey walk.

Dan warned Tracey that this kind of prostheses would be much harder to conquer and walk in because her stump was just all flesh. Without any bone there was really nothing left to move the leg except for the swinging of her hip. It was like sitting in a bucket that had a leg attached.

They strapped the leg tightly around Tracey's waist. She would then have to lift her hip up to pick the foot off the ground and then swing it forward. Then she would transfer all her weight onto the prosthesis so she could move her real leg.

Dan told Tracey that according to her size and strength it might take three to six months for her to walk independently. Then of course, he had to throw in the factors of determination and hard work.

When it came time for Tracey to try to walk she was more excited than a child waiting to open Christmas presents. They strapped the leg around her and adjusted it until she felt comfortable. There was still some tenderness where she had surgery so comfort wasn't completely attainable.

They placed Tracey between two parallel bars where she could support herself with her arms. Her knuckles were pure white as she clutched the bars with everything she had. After much instruction, Tracey was actually able to move herself down through the bars, doing it several times. Her face was just beaming with pride like a toddler that just took her very first steps. She said jokingly, "Okay, that was easy, what's next?"

Tracey did so well that Dan asked if she wanted to try to walk with crutches. Tracey's answer flew out of her mouth before he could even finish asking her.

"Yes, give me those crutches, I want to walk."

He told her this was going to be a lot harder because she would have to control her weight and balance even more on her own. Tracey didn't bother to listen to what he was saying. She didn't want to hear anything that might suggest she couldn't do it.

Tracey took off walking, making it seem easy. The determination factor Dan was talking about was kicking in right about then. Dan praised her and told her she was way ahead of the curve. He told Tracey to spend some time practicing with the crutches and then after she got proficient with them she could try walking with a cane.

Instead of being happy about doing so well, Tracey seemed to have a look of disappointment on her face. She asked, "Why can't I try to walk with a cane right now?"

Dan told her it wasn't a good idea to try to hurry her progress, she needed to learn to "walk before she could run." He said, "We don't want you to fall and hurt yourself." As he was speaking, I think he realized Tracey was not your average amputee, or person for that matter.

She responded with total sincerity, "I have been thinking about this day for a long time. I have already determined that I'm going to fall many times over the rest of my life but I am resolved to get back up every time I do. *It's not the fear of falling that concerns me; it's the fear of not getting back up that does.*"

Without any argument, Dan gave Tracey a cane saying, "Okay Tracey, go ahead and walk." It wasn't pretty or perfect by any means, but she walked. Her whole body shook as she struggled for the strength to take the next step. Nevertheless, there was no waver in her resolve. The look on her face defined the word determination.

Tracey's willpower united with God's power to help her to walk one step at a time. Tracey's one hand was grasping a cane but her other hand was holding on to God's. The cane gave her balance while God gave her strength. The cane was going to help her walk while God was going to help her live.

Tracey could walk because she wasn't afraid of falling or failing. Her focus was so intense the *fear of failure was never an option with her*. She knew that allowing herself to be consumed by fear would be even a greater handicap than missing a leg. She had seen so many people that couldn't even get out of bed or leave the house because of their bondage to fear; she wouldn't be one of them.

Tracey knew that pain usually accompanied falling. However, no pain was great enough to keep her from wanting to get back up and walk. Falling down would never make Tracey feel like a failure, but staying down would. Falling down was inevitable, but giving up was unacceptable.

Tracey believed God would not let her fail by falling, physically or spiritually. "The Lord delights in the way of the man whose steps he has made firm; though he stumble, he will not fall, for the Lord upholds him with his hand." (Psalm 37:23, 24)

Tracey didn't spend a long time on the crutches, she went on to walk very well with her new leg using her cane and walking slowly with a limp. Most people never realized she had an artificial leg and would frequently ask how she hurt it. Joey thought it was the coolest thing in the world, wanting to know why he couldn't take his off. It didn't take long for that leg to become part of Tracey. She was quite protective of it because it represented her mobility. It was so important that she be able to be as independent as possible by getting wherever she wanted to go. In other words, the leg gave her freedom.

Although the artificial leg performed well for her it still had its moments of imperfection, some even comical. She worked in downtown Akron where the traffic was busy during lunchtime. Tracey had to move as fast as she could to get across a four-lane street during a red light. One day, a storm was moving in and the wind was gusting well over thirty miles an hour. Tracey began to cross the street on her way back from lunch. When she was halfway across, the wind caught her leg and picked it up, holding it straight out to the side about waist length. At the same time, her dress flew over her head. Tracey tried frantically to pull it down while at the same time push her leg back down to the ground. Her wonderful balance helped to keep her standing on just one leg while all of this was going on.

It was so embarrassing for her but she had to admit the looks on the faces of the people she passed were hilarious. Their eyes got so big they almost popped out of their heads. Some were so scared they started to run away while others just held out their hands not knowing what or where to grab.

On numerous occasions, I would get phone calls from Tracey while she was at work. I could tell she was crying so right away I would think she fell or was hurt in some way. However, Tracey usually never cried about pain for she had an incredible tolerance to it. No, these phone calls were about feeling embarrassed or stupid.

In her haste to get to work, Tracey would sometimes forget to change the shoe on her artificial leg. She wouldn't notice until she got to work, realizing then that she had two different colors on. It wasn't earth shattering but she just felt there were certain things she could control, having the same color shoes on was one of them. I would take the right shoe to her staying only until I got her to laugh about it; it wasn't always that easy.

Worse than that, sometimes the bolt in the foot part of the leg would loosen, turning it completely around facing backwards. Again, I would hop in the car no matter what I was doing and go to the rescue. I was her "knight in shining armor" as long as I had an Allen Wrench in my hand.

Tracey's artificial leg enabled her to do almost anything others did. It just took a little more time and a lot more effort. Tracey was determined her performance at work would never be anything but excellent. Losing a leg to cancer was not an excuse to be lazy. In fact, most people found themselves struggling to keep up with her.

Chapter 16

Get Yourself Together

There were many ways to show my love for Tracey. However, the things I could do for her spoke way louder than anything I could ever say. Although Tracey was very independent, it was especially important to her that I take control when it came to dealing with the doctors and her medical care.

She knew I would ask a million questions and then go look for all the information I could get my hands on. I was determined to educate myself so I could better understand the information told to us. I wanted to be part of the decision-making, not just sit back, and do whatever we were told.

I trusted the doctors, but I never accepted them as being infallible, this whole thing started with a misdiagnosis because of a doctor's oversight. I just wanted to make sure there weren't any more. Tracey knew I would make sure she got the best of care. She might not have always liked my tactics, but she did the results.

I don't know if it's fair to say that Tracey lived in denial of what was happening but she did try to avoid any bad news. She had the kind of *metastatic disease* that could spread or come back at any time and she understood that. Therefore, she never called for any of the test results from her blood work or bone scans. She wanted me to call in case there was any bad news. This way she could hear it from me knowing I would explain things without ever taking away her hope. Tracey was all about hope.

We met with the oncologist who would be administering the chemotherapy. At that time, there was no one particular drug to use. He shared the various possibilities along with the differences between the drugs and their side effects. One of the drugs would more than likely cause her hair to fall out while another drug caused more nausea and sickness. There wasn't a clear choice, none of them was without side effects.

As he was talking, he said "Oh, by the way. You're not pregnant are you? I can't give you chemo if you're pregnant. It would harm the baby or probably abort the pregnancy. If you're not pregnant just make sure you're careful."

Deciding what medicine to use required similar consideration as whether to amputate or save the leg. Tracey was more concerned about the effectiveness of killing the cancer cells than how sick she would be, or look. The final decision was always with Tracey but my opinion carried a lot of weight in what she ultimately did. We decided to opt for what we thought to be the most aggressive approach. That sent us to look for wigs.

We looked at many styles but Tracey decided to try to match what was closest to her natural look. So many other changes were happening there was no reason to start changing her hairstyle; even with a wig. I wanted Tracey to get the best wig she could find. Money was no object; we would get a loan if we had to. I wanted her to feel comfortable when she had to start wearing the wig and not have to worry if it resembled "road kill."

A few days after talking with the doctor, Tracey told me she needed to talk with me. She could not stop thinking about what the doctor said about getting pregnant.

"Denny, I just can't get pregnant or even take the chance to. I have to take this chemo to make sure I can live. If I got pregnant after the chemo, I know I'd probably have to live in a wheel chair, my artificial leg wouldn't strap around my growing belly. Anyways, there's always the chance the cancer could come back and hurt the baby, or me. I've thought long and hard about it. I know we've always dreamed about having other children but I don't want to risk it, not now, not in this condition.

"Birth control pills or any other contraception is not safe enough for me to gamble on getting pregnant. I'm not sure how long I'll live so I would never ask you to get a vasectomy. Even if you did, I wouldn't trust it. If anything happened to me I would want you to still be able to have more children."

I realized Tracey was not rejecting me. It wasn't about me; it was about her and the cancer. I would have felt very selfish if I would not have understood and honored what Tracey was asking of me. I knew real love was putting your spouse's needs first. It was looking out for their best interests and not your own. Any sacrifice I needed to make paled in comparison to what Tracey had to do every day. We agreed abstinence would be the right decision for the rest of our marriage.

I would always go with Tracey for every chemo treatment or doctors visit. I never took anything for granted while overseeing everything. All the nurses loved Tracey but I was public enemy number one. They didn't like me questioning what they did or how they were going to do it. I guess I held them to a much higher standard than most people did. Don't get me wrong, I totally appreciated them, especially when they did everything right.

One day Tracey was getting her chemo and the nurse would not be quiet. She was more interested in telling us her personal stories than she was in doing her job. She was so bad even Tracey was getting annoyed with her, so you know what I was thinking. I kept asking if she was doing everything right since she didn't seem to be paying careful attention to Tracey. She just continued to tell another story.

About ten minutes into the treatment, I jumped up and yelled, "What's wrong with her arm, it's turning bright red?"

The nurse missed Tracey's vein so the highly toxic drugs were going into the tissues of her skin causing the reaction we were seeing. The nurse pulled out the needle immediately, any longer and there might have been permanent damage to the skin.

She didn't have much to say the rest of the time other than how sorry she was. This was just another reason why Tracey liked me to be with her when she was having things done to her. We forgave the nurse but never forgot what happened.

After taking a couple rounds of treatments, the side effects started coming, causing hair loss and severe nausea. Nevertheless, Tracey faced the adversities of chemo head on, never allowing them to stop her or even slow her down. She never missed work even though numerous hours were spent in the rest room getting sick. God was even giving her grace for the chemo treatments.

I'm not attempting to paint Tracey as a "super hero," just one tenacious woman.

After most of the trauma subsided our family was able to establish a more normal routine, at least what was normal to us. Tracey was getting around well and went back to work. I started to travel in my ministry again while Joey continued to act unscathed by everything that happened.

I did all the shopping and cooking as well as physically took care of Joey for most things. When I was out of town, Tracey's mom would come and stay at the house to help with

Joey and anything else needing done. Shirley learned how to be both a mom and best friend to her daughter, which drew them even closer. She was a tremendous help, I might not have been able to go out and share Jesus without her.

Tracey eventually started to drive again. If she had to lose a leg, at least it was her left one. The handicap didn't impair her in any way from her ability to drive as before, however the *jury is still out* on just how good that was. I guess you could call her a "magical driver" since she never looked at the road when driving. She spent most of the time looking in the rearview mirror while doing her makeup. I threatened more than once to tear it out. Tracey lost over thirty pounds from her surgery but her "lead foot" did not get any lighter.

Although Tracey got around very well with her prosthesis, there were times I needed to be her legs, especially in the mornings. Joey was already too big for Tracey to carry so that's where I stepped in. Every morning I would go into Joey's room and carefully pick him up without waking him. I would carry him into our room and place him into Tracey's waiting arms. Their two beautiful faces mirrored one another as they snuggled face to face. Tracey would gently kiss Joey's cheek numerous times until she felt satisfied that she got her "Joey fix" for the day.

Other than the Lord, Joey was Tracey's source of strength and happiness. He was her precious little lamb and her reason for getting up each day. *It wasn't the medicine and surgeries keeping Tracey alive, it was her love for Joey.*

While they snuggled, I would go into the kitchen and prepare Tracey's breakfast then serve her at the makeup table. I would kneel down from behind, put my arms around her shoulders and place my face beside hers where both were visible in the mirror. I would always say, "You see that girl in the mirror, she's the most beautiful girl in the world."

I'd say it every time, every day, always wanting her to feel special. I never allowed her to think she was less of a woman or wasn't beautiful. I knew it was most important that she hear it from me.

While eating, Tracey did her devotions praying and thanking God for one more day. After finishing her breakfast, Tracey would first do her makeup. She lost all her body hair from the chemo so the next step to beautifying herself would be to glue on her false eyelashes. After successfully getting them straight she would then put on her wig and comb it to make sure it was presentable. Then she would slip on her prosthesis followed by her clothes.

Sometimes I had to leave the room so she wouldn't see me crying. It was very hard for me to watch my wife have to literally "put herself together" just to face another day.

It would be ridiculous to believe it didn't bother Tracey. Some days were harder than others and being positive took a lot more effort. It wasn't easy for her to look into a mirror and see herself missing a leg and all her hair. It was through her devotions and prayers that she found the encouragement to go on. God's Word gave her both the strength and inspiration needed to accept what she saw in the mirror. The Bible is God talking and Tracey talked with him every day. No day was ever easy but each one had the potential of being special.

Chapter 17

Do I Really Need a Turn?

The next few years were good for Tracey. She healed from all the surgeries and seemed quite healthy. She was also doing very well at her job. The superior work she did completely overshadowed the fact she was handicapped, Tracey got upset if anyone referred to her as disabled. She said her leg slowed down her walking, not her brain. Losing her leg was never an excuse not to work hard; it motivated her to work even harder.

Tracey had routine check ups that included blood work, C.A.T. scans, and nuclear bone scans. Still, Tracey would have me call for the results. Getting to tell her there were no visible signs of reoccurrence was my most favorite thing to do. We always celebrated the happy news with a special dinner or something out of the ordinary.

Tracey set her sights on being cancer free for five years believing that if she got to that milestone she would have beaten the cancer completely. Tracey wasn't consumed with constant worry but she was still anxious about her future, especially with Joey.

Joey was about four years old now, a handsome lad if I might say so myself. I feel comfortable in saying that since he looks exactly like his mommy. He was really a good boy, high-spirited and strong willed, but obedient. It was hard sometimes to find the balance between breaking his will without damaging his spirit but I think I succeeded. I never allowed myself to feel sorry for Joey because his mommy was sick or different. I realized early on that no one, not even my baby boy, should have an excuse to misbehave or to be spoiled.

Although I might take some of the credit for Joey's good behavior, Tracey was responsible for a lot of his personality. Joey had a kinder side to him than most little boys his age. I believe growing up with a handicapped mommy caused Joey to be a more sensitive and compassionate person. He was always very gentle with his mommy and treated her with loving respect.

At the same time, Joey wasn't overly affectionate and seemed guarded with his emotions. He didn't cry much unless he was physically hurt or strongly chastised. Tracey always wanted to protect Joey by hiding her pain and suffering from him. Somehow, I believe he instinctively learned to hide his emotions in a similar fashion.

Even at four years old, I could tell by Joey's physique that he was going to be a good athlete. We were close buddies and we spent most of our time together playing some kind of sport. Although he was precious to Tracey, I knew he was still a *daddy's boy*.

Joey was bright and learned very fast so we decided to put him into pre-school. He got along well with other children and looked forward to going to school. While there, Joey said some things that amused the teacher, which she shared with me on different occasions.

One day, the subject of handicapped people came up so the teacher asked is anyone knew what the word handicapped meant. Joey raised his hand and when called on answered, "It's when someone does what other people can do but just slower." The teacher thought it was an interesting answer and asked if he knew anyone who was handicapped. Joey said proudly, "Yep, my mommy is. She only has one leg." Joey never acted ashamed of his mommy. He was proud of Tracey and their love for each other transcended anything else that might be missing.

The next day the teacher asked, "Who is the happiest person you know?" When it was Joey's turn, he responded, "My mommy is."

The teacher seemed surprised at his answer and asked "Didn't you say your mommy is handicapped?" Joey confirmed she was and the teacher started to cry, realizing what a wonderful example Tracey was to Joey.

It's funny how some people believe the only way someone can be happy is if they have a perfect life and everything they want.

One day Tracey parked in a handicapped spot in front of the grocery store. When she got out of the car, a woman came running up to her threatening to call the police because Tracey had parked there. Tracey was taken back at first, then almost apologetically told her she *was* handicapped. The woman didn't believe her so Tracey showed her artificial leg. The woman was so embarrassed and began to beg for forgiveness. She explained that she never thought anyone so pretty and so happy could be handicapped. Tracey took the opportunity to tell the woman that anyone can be happy no matter what the circumstance, as long as he or she knows Jesus.

One day while picking Joey up from school, his teacher asked if she could talk to me for a moment. At first, I thought he might have gotten in trouble but she went on to ask me what I did for a living. I told her I was a singer and a preacher. She started to laugh aloud and replied, "Well, I guess that makes sense."

"What makes sense?" I asked.

She proceeded to tell me that during their share time she asked the children what their daddy's work was. Joey's answer was "I don't know. He just tells people what to do and they do it." Wouldn't all preachers be glad if that were really true?

On the way home, I asked Joey why he said that in class. He answered, "When you say stand up, the people stand up. When you say sit down, they sit down. When you say sing, they sing. They do what you tell them to."

I got a lot of mileage out of Joey's observation and began most of my sermons by telling the congregations my four-year-old son told me to tell you that you have to do whatever I tell you to do.

We were all flying high during those times. Our household felt almost invincible since it seemed we had beaten cancer. However, that wasn't going to be the case. It was now Joey's and my turn to face our own health problems. It was time to put up our "spiritual dukes" and start fighting again.

One day I was trying to show Joey how to write the letters of the alphabet on a big chalkboard. I would print the letter "A" and then ask Joey to duplicate it. He wasn't even close to matching what I had shown him. After a dozen unsuccessful tries, I started to get aggravated with him and began to raise my voice. I was sure he wasn't paying attention or trying very hard, he was much smarter than that.

I drew a straight line, representing the left side of the capital "A" then asked, "Now, how many lines are there?"

Joey answered, "Two."

Now I thought he was trying to be funny or attempting to be a smart-aleck. I asked him again and warned him he better give the right answer. He took his finger and while pointing to the chalkboard counted "One, two."

I was now beside myself and shouted, "You're telling me that you see two lines?"

Joey started to cry as he counted again, "Yes daddy, one, two."

I made another line and then another and another and another. Joey's response was the same every time until it finally hit me that Joey must be seeing double. There was something wrong with his eyes and there I was yelling at him.

I took him in my arms and started crying myself, apologizing to him repeatedly. I felt so bad. He was trying so hard to please me but his little eyes were failing him. He later told me he knew I wanted him to say one, but he just couldn't tell a lie.

We took Joey to see Dr. Robert Burnstine, a specialist in Pediatric Ophthalmology. We heard great things about him and felt confident he was the man for the job. He told us Joey was seeing double because of a weak eye muscle. The eye was turning in slightly, causing it not to focus properly. He suggested we should first try patching it to force the eye to work harder, causing the muscle to strengthen.

Instead of getting better, Joey's eye became worse, turning inward until he stared at the bridge of his nose. Dr. Burnstine decided to operate because of the lack of progress. The surgery would entail tightening the muscle by removing a small segment to shorten it. It sounded routine the way Dr. Burnstine described it, but Tracey and I were still worried about our baby boy's beautiful brown eyes. Having part of your son's eye cut out was enough to cause anyone to be anxious. We turned our anxiety into prayer and believed God for the rest.

Joey went through the surgery with flying colors. It was probably best that he was so young, not knowing much of what was happening to him. He was so precious when he first came out of the anesthetic, although he looked as though he had been in a bad fight and lost, with his eye all swollen and filled with blood.

He was still kind of groggy and had a hard time sitting up on his own. As Tracey was dressing Joey to go home, I kept rubbing his back while telling him how proud I was of him and what a brave boy he was. He turned and looked straight at me with that bloody eye, saying quietly, "Shut up pig face!" Tracey and I both started laughing then quickly tried to contain ourselves. We didn't want Joey to think we were making fun of him or that what he said was okay. We knew it was the drug talking, at least that's what I hoped. I had no idea where those words came from but I guarantee he never said them again. This time he deserved a little grace.

Joey healed very quickly, his eye was perfectly straight. He never had another problem or ever had to wear glasses. We were very thankful for Dr. Burnstine and his masterful hands.

Then came my turn although I would have been fine to not get one. The years of nightclub singing as well as the preaching and singing in church was starting to take its toll on my voice. My motto was always the "show must go on," although it wasn't always the smartest thing to do.

There were many times when I was very sick and had no business preaching or singing, let alone even talking. I would still perform, putting a tremendous strain on my vocal chords. Through the years, I mastered how to sing with laryngitis by forcing my vocal chords to slam together. By doing this, I ended up with both nodules and polyps on my vocal chords. My voice became very raspy and at times I could barely talk. Not the best situation for a person who depends on his voice for a living.

I went to a nose and throat specialist to see what could be done. The doctor was reluctant to do surgery without first trying to reverse the damage through rest and speech therapy. I knew it wouldn't work but I went along with it, trying hard to do whatever he suggested.

Eventually, it became apparent that laser surgery was inevitable for me to get my voice back. I was putting my career in the hands of this surgeon while at the same time putting his hands into God's. I prayed very hard for my voice to be restored back to me, it was hard for me to imagine not being able to sing again.

I wasn't allowed to talk at all for almost two weeks after the surgery. Me not talking! Anyone who knew me thought it would take a miracle for that to happen. I even talk in my sleep. Tracey wasn't upset by it and Joey considered it to be the greatest gift he ever received.

I walked around with a note pad and had to write whatever I wanted to communicate. When I needed to correct Joey I would write in big bold letters pressing as hard as I could with the pencil. Although Joey couldn't always read what I what writing, he had no problem reading my expressions. I broke a lot of pencils during those two weeks.

After my checkup, the doctor told me it was okay to start talking again. I was excited but at the same time scared. I could only think, " Will my voice come back completely, will I ever be able to sing again?"

I took it slow, trying hard not to force anything. I was reluctant to sing or speak loudly for the fear of injuring myself again. I practiced singing around the house, but only songs that took little effort.

It didn't take long for me to realize that those songs weren't who I was. I had a big voice and never held back when I sang. I decided that I wouldn't concern myself any longer with how I sounded, just who was hearing it.

I was a little anxious the first opportunity I had to sing. During the song, I went after a high note and hit it perfectly. I was able to sing both the strong notes as well as the soft without a hint of raspiness. My vocal chords were completely healed, my voice was clear as a bell. My voice was back; I was back.

Both our surgeries seemed insignificant in comparison to Tracey's. Nevertheless, both were cause for concern and everyone around us rallied with their support. Every experience drew us closer as a family and to Jesus. They served not as distractions, but as constant reminders of our total dependence upon him.

Chapter 18

Speaking Out

Tracey had numerous opportunities for ministry over the five years following her amputation. Because of her job responsibilities, Tracey didn't always go with me to every church. She usually went when there was a specific request for her to share her testimony.

Tracey never felt the need to go for herself, it was hard on her to work all week then travel sometimes hundreds of miles over the weekend. Though people were very kind, it was difficult for her to relax in someone else's home. Our home was equipped with apparatus for her to shower as well as for other needs she had. The homes we traveled to could not be as accommodating.

At the end of each day, Tracey relaxed by taking off her prosthesis, moving around the house with her crutches. She didn't feel comfortable doing this in front of others so her day seemed extra long when she wore her leg for its entirety. Still, Tracey was willing to sacrifice her comfort if it meant she got the chance to share Jesus.

Many people did receive help or inspiration from Tracey's testimony. She wasn't a preacher, yet her life was a convicting sermon to some and a message of healing to others. There are a few stories that particularly come to mind.

On one occasion, a woman approached Tracey after she had given her testimony. The woman was very serious, asking if she could talk to her privately. She shared with Tracey that she had a form of muscular dystrophy since childhood. Hearing Tracey speak made her feel ashamed of herself.

The woman could never come to grips with her disease, choosing to be bitter instead of accepting what life had dealt her. She confessed that she was unable to see what others might need because of focusing so much on her own problems. She almost didn't come to hear Tracey fearing the conviction she might feel.

She was a Christian, but allowed her disease to be an excuse for not getting involved in church. Even when there was something she knew she could do, she would say she was unable to do it. She put up a wall so other people wouldn't try to approach her. Doing so caused others to think of her as unfriendly and insensitive, resulting in a life of loneliness.

She went on to tell Tracey that seeing another handicapped person so happy and praising Jesus made her search deep inside of herself. When she did, she realized her heart needed more of a touch from Jesus than her diseased body. She realized how she wasted most of her life being angry, instead of using it to serve God. She promised to spend her remaining years being involved in other people's lives, but asked how God could use her.

Tracey shared with the woman that no physical handicap should ever dictate one's ability to love. As long as she was willing to love people, God would show her a way to serve. God was not as concerned with what she could or couldn't do but more with what she was willing to do. Sometimes, when there is a will, there is a way.

Another time, a young woman in her early twenties came forward during the invitation. When she arrived at the altar, she stood for a brief moment then collapsed onto her knees with all of her weight. I was afraid she might have hurt herself.

After praying with several others, I knelt to pray with her. She was crying very hard with her face buried in her arms where I couldn't see it. I spoke to her various times but there was no response. I wasn't sure if she wanted to be left alone or if she was embarrassed.

When she finally raised her head, I found myself looking into one of the most beautiful faces I had ever seen. She had long blonde hair and eyes that were bluer than blue. Her complexion was flawless except for the mascara streaming down her face. I asked her, "What do you want Jesus to do for you tonight?"

She answered by saying, "I don't know, I just need help."

I told her I was willing to help but she needed to tell me a little more so I would know how to pray for her.

She began to open up. "For my entire life, all I've ever been told was how pretty I am. I've been in beauty contests ever since I was a little girl and just recently was a finalist in my state contest for Miss America. I didn't do it for myself; I did it for my family and friends, so they would love me and be proud of me.

"No one ever tells me I'm nice or that I'm smart, just beautiful. They tell me I'll never want for anything because of my good looks. It makes me think people only like me or accept me for what I look like, without ever getting to know who I really am. Maybe it's because I don't even know who I really am. They don't realize that when I look in the mirror, I don't see someone beautiful. It's like looking at a picture that has only one expression and no life to it. I can only see myself as an empty shell because that's what I feel like inside.

"I have done so many stupid things in my life just so I could feel loved by a man, but no one ever loved me for me. What am I going to do?"

I asked her if she was listening to Tracey when she shared her testimony. She confirmed that she had; it was what Tracey said that caused her to come forward.

"Your wife is so beautiful. I want that same kind of beauty. She said she felt whole even though she was missing a leg. I want to feel whole like your wife, not empty anymore. I want to be loved the way you love your wife."

I responded by saying, "Jesus already loves you that much and even more. And he's waiting for you to fall in love with him. All the men you've tried to find love with were willing only to take from you. Jesus wants to show you what he is willing to give to you. He was willing to die for your sins so you could spend *eternity with him, not just one night.* There is no greater love than that. If you will ask him to come in, I guarantee you will never feel empty again. Would you like to do that right now and start feeling as beautiful as Tracey does?"

She accepted my invitation to pray and asked Jesus to come into her heart and save her. It was hard to believe, but she looked even more beautiful afterwards.

In 1991, a church in Canfield, Ohio asked Tracey and I to perform a concert for their church. They said they were praying very hard for a young man in their church and wanted him to be able to hear Tracey's testimony. He and his family were going through very hard times and needed a lot of encouragement. This young man was Dave Dravecky.

Dave Dravecky had been a major league baseball pitcher for the San Francisco Giants. In 1988, Dave found he had cancer in his pitching arm. He underwent surgery with the prognosis he might never pitch again. After the surgery, Dave trained hard to one-day pitch again, wanting to prove the doctors wrong.

On August 10, 1989, Dave defied all odds by not only pitching again, but also winning a game described by most as only miraculous. Five days later, Dave pitched again, but for the last time. During one of his pitches, Dave's arm broke so loudly people sitting in the stands even heard it.

Over the next couple of years, Dave endured multiple surgeries as well as radiation treatments with the intent of trying to save his arm. Dave and his wife Jan courageously battled the cancer, dealing with their own personal bouts of depression and suffering. In June of 1991, Dave and his doctors decided that his arm required amputation. Tracey and I met him soon after his surgery.

Both Tracey and I watched eagerly as everyone entered the sanctuary. We were hoping Dave would come as we both looked forward to meeting him. We were there to minister to everyone, but we especially wanted to be an encouragement to him. As Dave walked into the service, I couldn't help but notice the grave look on his face. It was hard to discern what he was thinking or feeling since we didn't know him. It didn't matter though, Jesus knew.

In our concert, we both sang individually as well as some duets together. One of our favorite songs to sing was *I've Just Seen Jesus*. That song contains one of the most potent lines you'll ever hear; *"I've just seen Jesus, and I'll never be the same again."*

Tracey started sharing her testimony beginning with her own bout with cancer. She shared how Jesus helped her to accept her amputation, giving her hope even in the darkest times. Tracey finished by proclaiming some of the most powerful words one amputee could say to another; "I may have only one leg, but it's planted on the *Solid Rock*."

After Tracey finished speaking, I gave an invitation to those needing prayer. Dave came forward and knelt at the altar. I asked him what he wanted God to do for him. Dave answered with such earnestness, "I want to be as strong as Tracey. I want that same kind of strength."

I shared with Dave that Tracey was half his size but possessed a spiritual strength the size of a mountain. It wasn't the physical size or gender that measured one's spiritual strength, but the magnitude of their faith that did.

Dave went on to share his desire to stay faithful to whatever the Lord had planned for his life. Our conversation ended with prayer, asking God to give Dave the strength he needed.

Dave and Tracey had a lot in common. Yes, both of them battled cancer, and both experienced the amputation of a limb. Most of all, they both knew Jesus. However, there was one major difference. Dave's cancer knocked him off the pedestal he was already standing on, while Tracey's cancer was lifting her onto a pedestal she had never known. On a given Sunday, millions of people could have watched Dave Dravecky pitch via television. As a pitcher, every eye focused on the brilliant arm that put him there. Losing his arm meant losing his career and his audience. Tracey's audience was only beginning.

It didn't take long for God to put Dave back on top of his pedestal. In my opinion, his audience is now more significant than what baseball ever gave him. Dave and Jan have written many books such as "Comeback" and "When You Can't Come Back." Their story has touched thousands of people. They now live in Colorado where Dave is president of "Outreach of Hope"; a ministry designed to help hurting people who are struggling with cancer or amputation.

That night was special for Tracey. Thinking she might have been an encouragement to Dave Dravecky helped add purpose to her ministry. However, Dave was no more special than the smallest child that Tracey might have inspired.

Tracey proved you didn't need to be a "superstar" to be used by God.

Chapter 19

The Truth Hurts

Tracey continued to overachieve at her job. Her ability to be a successful professional increased her feeling of independence as well as her sense of normalcy. Focusing on her daily work schedule kept her from thinking about anything physical. Some people think of their jobs as sheer drudgery, Tracey considered hers a haven of escape. She loved the place where she worked and made some close friends while there.

However, Tracey started to get antsy and began to look for bigger challenges. When another agency, *Marcus Advertising*, offered Tracey a position she struggled with the decision whether or not to leave. Two companies were now competing for her and it was a definite ego boost.

It wasn't about money; both were willing to match each other's offer. It was about growing and the opportunity to do so. Tracey asked for my opinion so I helped her make a list of pros and cons for each company. Regardless of what I thought, the final decision needed to be hers. She was going to have to be there every day. My biggest concern was Tracey having to drive an extra 30 miles each way if she made the change.

The final decision was to take the new job, but she didn't burn any bridges. There was a mutual respect between Tracey and all her associates. I don't believe anyone felt as though Tracey was turning her back on them only that she was just turning her face toward something new. I'm really not sure why she left, but she prayed about it for a long time. She felt a real peace about her decision and that was good enough for me.

About the same time, I was making some important decisions of my own. I was getting more of a burden for the local church and the area around my own town. I started to meet with Pastor Charlie and the conference superintendent about planting a church in an area just north of our church.

We spent time studying the demographics of that area and believed it was a prime place to start a new church. The plan consisted of Cornerstone mothering the church with a core group of families either living in that part of town or having a burden for the church plant.

After making the decision to proceed, I searched for a home in the center of that area, eventually finding a home where the rooms all flowed into one. This open design was good for having meetings until we grew out of it. The house was also on one level, which would be much easier for Tracey to get around.

I wrote a contract on the home and it was accepted. Our new home would also serve as a new church, and that was exciting. We were thrilled about all the changes taking place in our lives, believing God to be at the center of everything.

Tracey was now close to completing five years of being cancer free. It's the general consensus that if you make it for that amount of time your odds of beating the cancer are greatly in your favor. Tracey was getting excited and we even talked of having a big party to celebrate. We didn't want to be premature with our celebration but it looked as though she was going to make it.

Up to this point, all of her tests had shown no active tumors or visible cell activity. There was a problem though; we weren't scanning her body from head to toe.

One morning as I was delivering Tracey's breakfast to her, I found her rubbing her forehead with a concerned look on her face.

"What's the matter?" I asked.

Tracey answered, "There's a lump on my forehead and I don't know what it is. It's been there awhile but I really didn't pay much attention to it until it seemed to get bigger."

She asked me to look to see what I thought it was. I shined the lamp directly on her face so I could see well. She was right. There was a small lump at the top of her forehead, just under the hairline. I asked if I could touch it and upon doing so inquired if it hurt. There was no pain at all so I really didn't know what to make of it.

Neither of us wanted to say the word tumor. We could only speculate, thinking she might have bumped her head or had an infection of some sort. Somehow, deep down inside I think we both knew what it was. I tried to play it down but told Tracey we had still better go to the doctor and have it looked at more thoroughly.

We went to the doctor and the first thing out of his mouth was that it looked like a tumor. I understand oncologists deal with bad news all the time and their failure rate with patients is great. I just wish there was a more sensitive way of telling someone such bad news, but maybe there isn't.

Right away, I would jump in and say "But we can't be sure yet, can we?" The doctor would always agree that there was a possibility they were wrong. I just wanted Tracey to be able to hold on to her hope even if for only an extra minute.

Unfortunately, the doctor was right. It was the same bone cancer, only now in her skull. The C.A.T. scan revealed a tumor had eaten its way completely through the skull. On one side, it was pushing out against her skin where we could visibly see the lump. On the other side, it was invading the frontal lobe of her brain.

There are not as many nerve endings in the skull area so Tracey didn't feel any pain that would alarm her. If it wasn't for the bump on her head, we might not have known the tumor was even there. The next step was obvious. We needed to find a neurosurgeon and get this tumor removed, the sooner the better.

Tracey was referred to Dr. Ghassan Khayyat, a highly respected surgeon in our area. Tracey liked Dr. Khayyat almost immediately. He was very gentle with her and talked to her as though he was working with his own daughter. Tracey felt confident that she was in good hands.

The doctor was very precise in his explanation of the surgery. First, He would remove the tumor. Then, a large piece of Tracey's skull would be removed, enough to make sure there were clean margins. Next, a plate would replace the bone taken out.

As Dr. Khayyat was finishing, Tracey's eyes started to fill up with tears. He noticed her crying and compassionately said, "Don't be afraid, I promise not to hurt you. It's my job to make you better."

Tracey replied in a sobbing voice, "I'm sorry, it's not that I'm afraid. I just thought I was done with this, now it's starting all over again."

Tracey was so disappointed. She was always so high but now she couldn't have felt any lower. The same emotions from five years before were resurfacing. The fears and questions we had were all too familiar. It would have been normal for us to ask "Why again, God," but we believed he wanted to be trusted more than questioned. Neither one of us felt that it was right in getting mad at God. Why would we allow ourselves to be angry with the One we needed and depended upon most?

Once again, Tracey would have to dig deep to muster up the strength to face yet another surgery. Besides dealing with the pain, she would have half her head shaved and lined with stitches. Again, her faith was tested. However, she knew she served a big God who was able to see her through just as before.

She nestled herself in the bosom of Jesus as she drew closer to him in prayer. Many times when we prayed together, Tracey would repeat these words, "Jesus, I can face the surgeries and I'm willing to accept the pain. Please just let me live to raise my little boy." She could handle missing a leg or having a hole in her head as long as it meant just one more day with Joey. Living was what mattered most.

Tracey was determined not to give in to cancer, refusing to entertain the thought that it might take her life. It was her belief that negative thoughts just might help the cancer cells grow so she always tried to focus on the positive. Most doctors would probably argue with her theory but it wasn't a bad way to live.

My response was different. I'm a man of faith, but nevertheless I'm still a realist. I know many people believe a realist is a sanctified name for a pessimist, but I beg to differ. I believe a person can expect the best while preparing to accept the worst.

God has given us wonderful brains to use and there are times our intelligence lets us know what the outcome will be, aside from a miracle. God wants us to be obedient with what he has already given us rather than constantly giving us more. To stand firm in the middle of a battle shows far more character than seeking a way of retreat. Someone once said, "God will not do by miracle that which can be accomplished by obedience." Miracles will lead people to seek Jesus, but obedience will help them find him.

I was Tracey's husband, Joey's daddy, and a caregiver for both. As the spiritual leader of my home, I needed to demonstrate my faith, expand my mind, and strengthen my back. I asked God to prepare my heart for the future as I studied to prepare my mind for the present. Unlike Tracey, I asked the doctors to give it to me straight. I had already spent many hours studying the disease Tracey had and I wanted to confirm my findings with them. I felt I could better serve my family if I used my brain to understand how I could.

In reality, the cancer really didn't come back; it never left. Appearing somewhere else in the body was a confirmation that there were probably satellite cells throughout her whole body. It takes millions of cells to form even a small tumor and until the cells have multiplied to form such tumors, the cancer goes undetected. The chemotherapy might have slowed down the rate of cell growth but it obviously didn't eliminate them. *It was the same fight, only a different round.*

Understanding all of that, I talked with the doctors we worked with asking each one directly "Is my wife going to die?" Knowing me the way they did, none felt they had to try to protect me from the truth. They knew the truth would help me help Tracey.

The answer was "Yes, in all probability she is going to die." They felt sure the cancer was throughout her body and just a matter of time until it spread to her lungs or other vital organ.

I asked the obvious, "How long will she live?"

No one knew for sure or could even speculate at that time. As long as the cancer stayed in the bone and didn't metastasize into the lungs or any other vital organs, Tracey would more than likely stay alive. Cancer, while contained in the bone, would cause tremendous pain but it would probably not take her life.

The plan would be to try to keep up with the spreading tumors through surgery, chemotherapy, and radiation. The reality was it would be like a dog chasing its tail and never catching it. The tumors would always be one step ahead.

After speaking to the doctors, the first thing I did was to get alone with God. I understood that according to the medical prognosis Tracey was going to die, however I needed to know what God would say or do about it. After spending a lot of time telling God what I wanted to happen, I then quietly listened to hear what he had to say.

God's answer was so clear to me. As I closed my eyes, God showed me through a vision that Tracey was going to die. There would be no miracles, no healings in fact the pain would get worse instead of better. However, I felt at peace as God revealed that he would always be as near as he was right then. *The presence of the Holy Spirit overshadowed the absence of a miracle.*

Some skeptics might say that God really didn't speak to me or show me those things. It's hard to believe what you don't understand and even harder to understand when you don't believe. God has a plan when he decides to speak intimately with someone. How they respond helps carry out that plan. God speaks to many people, but he isn't always heard. He's not always heard because not everyone recognizes his voice or is willing to listen.

God showed me the future because he knew I would take better care of Tracey if I did know. He understood that I would have more patience and be more compassionate if I realized Tracey was going to die. I reminded myself of the words I promised, "For better for worse...till death do us part." God needed me to be a much stronger man than what I was if I was going to help fulfill his plan for Tracey. Part of that plan was for Tracey to live her life in such a way that she would continue to witness long after she was gone. This book is fulfilling a piece of that plan.

I needed to listen closely as God continued to speak. I knew I couldn't do this on my own. I needed *"someone to watch over me"* so I could watch over my family.

Now that we were going to be fighting cancer again, I knew I would not be able to dedicate enough time to plant a new church. What I thought was God's design might have been more of my own plan. I might have gotten ahead of God and allowed my zealousness to blind me. Nevertheless, now was not the time.

I spoke with the realtors and explained the situation. They were most gracious, the owners of the home let us out of the contract. They were very understanding and we appreciated their act of kindness so much.

Almost everyone goes through a time of grieving after a death, *but I started to grieve while Tracey was still alive.* It was so painful to watch her live while knowing she was going to die. I was suffering inside, but couldn't show it outwardly. My emotions had to stay bottled up to protect Tracey and Joey as well as her family. I would never do or say anything that would hinder the hope Tracey had. She wanted to live and nothing or no one was going to convince her she wasn't, not even cancer.

Tracey even shut out the doctors when they alluded to how serious her condition was. I knew one day Tracey would have to face reality, but it would be when she was ready and not a second before. I knew I had to be the one to tell her she was going to die. *Until then, I would wear a mask of hope while bearing a heart of grief.*

I intended this book to be more about Tracey and her tremendous courage. However, through writing this book, especially this chapter, I'm forced to relive all that happened, remembering just how painful it was. In looking back, I'm reminded how hard it was for me to know that my wife was dying yet continue to live each day as though she was not.

It was difficult to help everyone continually reach for something when I knew it really wasn't there. What I knew stayed with me except for a few close friends. I opened my heart to my pastors, Charlie and Brenda Young. Mostly, my conversations with Brenda helped me stay the course. Even after thirteen years, I can still feel some of the hurt. I hope I can leave most of the pain on these pages.

Chapter 20

No Sacrifice Is Too Big

My least favorite place in the world was a hospital yet I found myself sitting in a waiting room once again. The surgery on Tracey's skull wasn't expected to be as intense as her leg amputation, but we still had cause for concern. All the prayers and positive thoughts seemed to help but not as much as the surgeon's words, "The surgery went fine, she's going to be all right."

I never knew what to expect when I walked into the recovery room. I always prepared myself to see Tracey writhing in pain and looking beat up from surgery. Again, that wasn't the case.

I heard a lot of commotion as I walked into the room. There was Tracey, laughing and joking with all the nurses. I asked one of them how Tracey was doing and she responded, "Oh, she's doing fine. She's been entertaining us. Your wife is something else!" Tracey asked the nurses for a mirror and after seeing her head started calling herself the *Bride of Frankenstein*. Tracey continued to crack jokes about her new look and was keeping the nurses in stitches. It was hard to determine who had more, Tracey's head or the nurses.

Eventually, everyone received an admonishment to quiet down. The other patients were not feeling quite as cheery when coming out of their anesthetic.

The nurses were right. Tracey was "something else." She just woke up from having a large piece of her head removed but was still chirping like a happy little lark. Tracey seemed to exemplify the meaning of "true grit." How could someone so weak continually be so strong?

I wrote a song that helps to answer that question. The chorus says, *"I'm the strongest in my weakness, because of your sufficient grace. I stand the tallest in your presence when I fall down on my face. And though the thorns of life keep piercing me, in my worst I'll see your best. I'm the strongest in my weakness."*

Tracey felt bad because she was already missing time at her new place of employment. She had only been there a short time. To her, missing work was synonymous with being sick so she wanted to get back as soon as possible. She insisted on having her surgery on a Friday so she could use the weekend for recovery days. Tracey only missed two days of work from the surgery. She astonished everyone when she went strolling back into the office. Most people asked why in the world she was there or even how. She told them she felt fine and that it was boring sitting at home.

After the surgery, Tracey started chemotherapy again, as well as radiation treatments to her skull. We changed oncologists, working this time with Dr. Esther Rehmus. She told Tracey she could only have one more round of *Adriamycin*. This was the drug used on Tracey when she first had chemotherapy five years previously but she had maxed out on it. If she took any more it might cause damage to her heart. Of course we didn't want Tracey to incur any damage to her heart but the news was disappointing. We believed this drug worked well on her cancer. We would have liked to continue using it.

Dr. Rehmus conferred with our primary doctor, Dr. Leeson, and came up with a new combination of drugs she felt would be aggressive enough to help retard the tumors.

Tracey's veins started becoming worse and worse. The nurses were finding it hard to locate good veins for the intravenous needles. One night, Tracey began to cry when a nurse couldn't find a vein. The constant digging and probing started causing a lot of pain. I asked the nurse to dismiss herself and find someone else to try. Nurse after nurse tried but without success.

By this time, Tracey was really crying and I was getting very angry. I couldn't believe she needed to go through this much pain just to get a needle put in her arm. Now, no one wanted to try for fear of hurting her again. Tracey even asked me to stand out in the hall because she thought I was making the nurses nervous.

Amy, a young nurse I had known since she was a little girl, came in and asked Tracey if it was okay if she tried. She was also a Christian so she asked if they could pray before attempting to put in the needle. After saying a short prayer, Amy slipped the needle right into the vein her very first try. Tracey was so relieved and able to stop her crying. That night Amy was definitely an angel of mercy sent from heaven.

Because of what happened that night, a *MediPort* was surgically put into Tracey's chest so the drugs could be administered directly through it.

The chemotherapy Tracey was taking not only destroyed the cancer cells, but also attacked the good ones. The drugs can't discriminate between the two. Tracey's blood counts would become increasingly low after regimens of chemo.

Our doctor gave us a prescription for *Neupogen*, a new drug that was on the market. *Neupogen* caused the white blood cells to regenerate at a accelerated rate which would help eliminate the danger of infections, as well as decrease the time between chemo treatments. I was overwhelmed when I picked up the prescription and found the cost of one prescription to be was over $1400.00. But it was worth it if it helped Tracey's counts to get stronger.

Another drawback was that it had to be injected into Tracey's leg with a syringe. Tracey was more than willing to allow me to do almost anything for her but she was not going to allow me to give her a shot. Fortunately for Tracey, our next door neighbor, Terri McGlone, was a registered nurse and also a good friend.

Tracey needed the shots after each chemo treatment. So, every night for about a week, Terri would stop over after work to give Tracey an injection. Although Tracey felt a little awkward having a friend do it she really appreciated Terri's help and was blessed to have a friend so kind.

Tracey was constantly being x-rayed along with other scans of all types. One of the tests showed there was another tumor growing along the edge of the plate in Tracey's head. Here we were again, back in the hospital to have even more of her skull removed. Still, Tracey tried to stay as positive as she could. No one ever held onto hope as tightly as she did although it became harder and harder as time progressed.

Now, instead of taking years the bad news was coming within months of each other. Tracey's other hip started to hurt so we immediately went to a neurologist for an examination. He suggested multiple reasons why Tracey's leg was hurting, one of them being the possibility of cancer. When we pressured him for his honest opinion he offered, "Cancer would be the first thing to consider since you already have it in other areas of your body. If it walks like a duck, well you know the rest."

The tests were positive. The cancer was now throughout her entire hip and pelvic area. Dr. Leeson told us that to try and remove the affected area would leave Tracey without anything to support her bodyweight. There would be nothing there to hold her frame together. We decided to treat the cancer with strong doses of radiation, trying to shrink the tumors before considering surgery.

What Dr. Leeson had to say next was devastating to Tracey. He told her she couldn't take the chance of her hip or pelvis breaking, so she should avoid putting any stress on those areas by walking. This news was just as bad as being told she had cancer.

Tracey asked, "Are you telling me I have to stay in a wheelchair?"

Tracey knew the answer to that question before she even asked it. It was as though she was in shock or having a bad dream. Confining Tracey to a wheelchair was like putting her into prison and throwing away the key. Taking away her mobility was like stripping her of her independence. This meant Tracey would now have to be even more dependent on me. She loved that she could depend on me, but hated that she had to. She found herself resenting me for the very things she loved me for.

All this led to one of the biggest disagreements we experienced during our whole marriage. When Tracey's pain got really bad I told her she was going to have to quit her job. She shouted, "There's no way that I'm going to quit!"

I asked her how she thought she was going to get there. Suddenly, she realized she would not be able to get her wheelchair up and down the stairs or in and out of the car to drive herself. She was no longer able to even transport herself from the car seat into the wheelchair without putting too much weight on her hip.

She got so mad and started screaming at me, "Then you'll just have to take me!"

I told her I wasn't going to quit ministering to become her chauffeur. I would have to drive 40 miles to take her there and then 40 miles back. I would have to repeat the same drive to go back and get her at the end of the day for a total of 160 miles a day. There would be no time for me to work or do anything else for that matter.

I told Tracey we would find someone to stay with her while I tried to take more meetings or even get another job. Tracey got even angrier and began hurling sarcastic remarks challenging my ability to make as much money as her. She continued to say even more demeaning things about my ability to provide for us.

I was both angry and hurt at the same time. I said, "Tracey, you better realize right now that I'm still the best friend you have. You need me now more than ever. You know you cannot do this without me. I refuse to allow you to treat me this way and I will not be your whipping post. You are only thinking of yourself and your own feelings right now. Believe me; this is happening to all of us, not just you."

Then I left.

While I was gone, I spent the time thinking about what just happened. I hurt for Tracey but found myself *licking my own wounds*. I realized that Tracey was desperate and felt trapped, thinking her only escape was to lash out and fight. I was sure she didn't mean those things but I also knew it couldn't continue.

When I got back home, I found Tracey sitting quietly right where I had left her. The wheelchair was still in the car therefore she had no way to get anywhere. I felt horrible but kidded her by saying, "That's what you get." I think the situation made her realize just how dependent she really was on me. I didn't like the circumstances any more than Tracey did, but it was what we were stuck with.

She started crying as she said, "Denny, I'm sorry for saying all those things. You've been the best husband and father any man could be. I never meant to hurt you, I was so wrong to suggest that you couldn't take care of us; you do every day.

"I need you to understand that if I stop working I'll feel like I quit living. I fear if I stop moving I'll start dying. Except for being Joey's mommy, working is one of the only things that help me feel normal; I feel I'm failing at that too. I'm asking you to please help me continue to work so I can feel like I have a life. Please, don't take that away from me."

I was sympathetic to what Tracey was asking of me but wasn't sure I could grant her request. I knew if I agreed to transport her back and forth to work I would have to place my life on hold. I was also allowing my ego to get the best of me. I thought people would think I was less of a man to let my handicapped wife work while I served as her chauffer and a stay at home dad. I found myself doing exactly what I accused Tracey of doing, thinking only of myself.

I wasn't able to hear God through Tracey's barrage of demands or criticisms. His quiet voice was hard to hear in the midst of all the yelling and arguing. It was only through Tracey's quiet pleading that I began to hear God speak.

He reminded me that driving Tracey to work would not last for the rest of my life, *only for the rest of hers*. God made me realize this was a small sacrifice to make if it allowed Tracey to live out the rest of her life with dignity and purpose. It became obvious to me I had no greater ministry at that time than to help ensure the quality of Tracey's life. Never again would I consider it a burden, only a privilege.

Chapter 21

Straight from the Heart

*O*ur lifestyle was changing again but we were able to adapt and make it happen. At first, the drive back and forth to Tracey's job was monotonous, but I kept reminding myself of why I was doing it.

It didn't take very long for us to realize we needed a different vehicle. Tracey was disappointed that we had to trade in the sports coupe she had for a bigger sedan. Nevertheless, we needed a car with a large enough trunk to facilitate her wheelchair. A larger car would also provide more room to get in and out as well as more comfort for Tracey as she dealt with the pain in her hip.

I had too much time on my on my hands throughout the day and I began to go buggy. I tried to think of something I could do where I could be in control of my time and be productive. Another concern was to be able to involve Joey in something that would also be interesting to him. Joey needed to be with me, especially with what was happening.

The three of us put our heads together and came up with a great idea. For years, Joey and I had been investing in sports trading cards. We both loved sports but Joey knew more about the players and their stats than I did. We already had enough of an inventory to start our own shop, so we did. I guess you could say I was the financier and he was the brain. I may regret ever writing this.

Tracey said, "Since you guys are such sports nuts, why don't you name the store Sports Nuts?" Joey and I loved the name, so we agreed to use it. We added a little twist by spelling it *"Sports Nutz."* We rented a facility near to where we lived. This way, I could always be close to the business as well as home. With a small amount of money and just a little foresight, we were now a father and son business; or maybe I should say, the odd couple?

Tracey was the expert in advertising, so I yielded to her expertise for a way to promote ourselves. She had many ideas but one of them was far better than the rest. She suggested we call Dave Dravecky to see if he would be interested in coming for our grand opening. What a tremendous idea!

I heard Dave was really doing great so I called him and explained our situation. He was more than gracious and agreed to come for our grand opening. He brought his books along with him, incorporating a book signing as part of the event. Tracey made sure the local newspapers knew about Dave's coming and they showed up to cover the occasion. People lined up in long lines just to get a chance to meet Dave Dravecky and get his autograph.

The day was a great success. We could not have had a better introduction of our shop to the public. A photo appearing in the local newspaper captured the most memorable part of the day. It was a picture of Dave and Tracey sitting together at a table with him signing autographs. Most people might have seen two amputees when they viewed the photo. Anyone who knew them saw much more. They recognized the silent admiration and respect they had for one another, they shared a bond only the two of them could realize.

Dave's willingness to help touched Tracey's heart. She knew deep down he did it more for her than anything else. Although no one spoke of Jesus that day, he was still visible through the living witness of these two courageous people. *Sometimes our scars speak louder than anything our lips could ever say.*

Times of fun and excitement were now short lived in our household. A chest x-ray revealed a tumor growing in Tracey's lung. The battle became more intense than ever and it came time to confront our greatest fears. As long as her lungs stayed clean, I knew Tracey had a chance for an extended life. The doctors could only strategize on how to prolong Tracey's life rather than how to save it.

This latest news created a sense of urgency in my spirit. I felt we were drowning in a sea of hopelessness and the doctors were literally out of life preservers. The grieving process that had started years before was crushing my spirit. I found it hard to pray and I begged God for the grace to go on autopilot. I likened myself to a jet that had run out of fuel but still had people to carry. I could only hope to glide the rest of the way supported by the powerful wind of God's Holy Spirit. I trusted God completely for only he knew where and when we would land.

They scheduled a biopsy of the tumor in Tracey's lung. I was totally against it because everyone already knew what it was. It seemed as though we had become robotic, just following a protocol that was hurting Tracey more than comforting her. I wanted to tell Tracey to refuse the biopsy, but I couldn't. I knew she would have interpreted it as giving up.

They shoved a large needle into Tracey's side that collapsed her lung. They were trying to align the needle with the tumor so they could get a piece of it to test. They were able to watch everything on a sophisticated system as they worked. I wasn't impressed by the technology, all I could see was the hurt it caused Tracey and her ability to resist pain was diminishing.

Several times, I almost made them abort the test. I felt like tackling the technician as Tracey's eyes kept begging for help. I stood helpless as I watched the tears run down her face. How much more did this little girl have to endure?

A few days later Tracey was lying on the couch in our upstairs living room still recovering from the traumatic experience. As I walked into the room I asked, "Is there anything I can get you?" Tracey caught me off guard with her response. I was about to enter into the saddest conversation I had ever had in my life; or ever will.

In a quiet, inquisitive voice Tracey asked, "Denny, I'm going to die soon, aren't I?" Before I could even think of how to respond she added, "Please be honest with me, I don't want to pretend anymore."

It's amazing how in just a few moments the human brain can compute hundreds of thoughts with none of them being the one you're really looking for. It seemed obvious by Tracey's statement this wasn't the first time she thought about dying, although it was the first time she allowed herself to say it.

I had thought about this moment countless times, however nothing could have actually prepared me for it. She asked for my honesty. She deserved nothing less. While shaking my head, I answered only, "Yes."

I thought I should go to her and hold her but I waited. Somehow, I knew Tracey needed to purge herself of all the emotions she was experiencing. I just stood in the center of the room, only listening as Tracey began to speak.

"I knew it. I just didn't want to believe it. I needed to hear you say it. It just seemed easier not to accept it. Why should everyone be sad? I couldn't be happy if all I thought about was dying. If I lost hope, no one would have seen Jesus. It kept me going each day. I would have let my whole family down, especially Joey.

"I want Joey to always remember that his mommy never gave up hope. When he's faced with struggles in his life I want him to remember what I went through, that I never quit. I don't want him to ever give up. I want Joey to get back up every time he falls down.

"I wasn't trying to be strong for me, but for everyone else. I wanted to be a good example and make Jesus proud of me. I don't regret doing it this way. I would rather be happy ignoring reality than be sad accepting it. But I accept it now. I'm not afraid to die, I was just afraid I wouldn't get the living part right. I'm only telling you this now in case the time comes when I can't."

Many times, I wanted to respond to the things Tracey said. However, I knew if there was anytime to listen, it was then.

"Denny, I could never thank you enough for all you've done for me. You were truly that "someone to watch over me" as you always say. I am so blessed to have you. I know no other man who would have stuck it out with me the way you did, I guess you got much more than you bargained for when you married me. I'm sorry you got stuck with me. I'm sorry things had to end up this way but I'm truly not worried about you. I know you'll be all right. I know God will bless you because of what you did for me.

"I want you to know that I want you to get married again. You deserve to be happy and I don't want you grieving for me after I'm gone. Just because my life is going to end doesn't mean yours has to. I need you to be all right, not for me, not even for you, but mostly for Joey."

By this time I couldn't take anymore. My heart was breaking for her and I wanted to comfort her somehow. I wanted to tell her she didn't need to say all those things. As soon as I tried to open my mouth, Tracey said, "Let me finish. I need to get this all out."

Up to this point, Tracey had been very calm as she shared but her composure soon changed as she began to talk about Joey. She started to cry so hard she began to hyperventilate. She was having a total breakdown. I didn't know how to help her except to pray she got through this without hurting herself. Her words were almost unintelligible as she struggled to speak. Those haunting words still echo inside me as if I were still in the room listening all over again.

"I'm not afraid to die; sometimes I just wish I would. There's nothing to keep me here anymore except Joey. I'm tired of hurting, and I'm tired of all the tests and medicine. I'm tired of all the hospitals and doctors. I'm tired of acting happy when I'm supposed to be sad. Denny, I'm just so tired. I want to go home but I don't want to leave my little boy. Denny, I'm never going see Joey grow up!"

With those words, she started to become hysterical. I ran to her trying to calm her down by holding her trembling body and urging her to stop talking. She began to scream but I shouted even louder, "Tracey, please stop! Stop for at least awhile until you can calm down." I startled her by shouting so loudly. I was trying to divert her attention away from thinking about Joey but to no avail. She started to get mad at me but I said, "No! You have to stop. You're making yourself sick."

I started talking to her as calmly as I could, catching each tear as I caressed her cheek. I held her as if she was a little girl until all the whimpers seemed to subside.

Tracey began to speak again, only this time with more control. "Denny, I cherish every minute I've had with Joey but I'm not ready to let go. I'm going to miss so much of his life. I won't be there when he drives his first car for the first time so you better not yell at him too much.

"I'm not going to see Joey graduate from high school and go off to college. I'm never going to know what Joey will do for a living. I'll never know what he'll look like as a grown man, but I know he'll be beautiful.

"I'll never know any of Joey's girlfriends and I won't be there to help him pick out a wife, so you better make sure she's somebody I'd like. I won't be able to cry at his wedding because I won't be there. When he gets married, please tell him I would have been proud of him and would have cried.

"I'll never be able to hold Joey's babies or hear the words Grandma. Joey will never see me grow old.

"Denny, I don't want you to raise Joey by yourself. You're the best daddy in the world but Joey still needs a mommy. It makes me so sad to think he would call anyone else mom, but if I can't be his mommy then someone else needs to be.

"He needs a mommy who can run with him and play with him. Promise me you will marry someone who will fly a kite with Joey. I always wanted to go running through a field with Joey while flying a kite but I guess someone else will have to."

Unexpectedly, Tracey began to laugh as she quipped, *"I hate her already."*

Tracey finished by saying, "Denny, you have to promise me three things. The first is you'll always permit Joey to see my mom and allow him to be close with her. I know my mom will always keep my memory alive by talking about me with Joey.

"Second, promise me you'll work on your anger. I don't want Joey to have your temper when he grows up.

"Third, always love Joey enough for the both of us. Always remind him my favorite thing to say to him was *"I love you my son, I'll always love you."*

Tracey continued to live each day as though the conversation about dying never happened. She was determined that although her life might be ending, her fight was not. She was not ready to give up by giving in. Tracey realized she needed to have the same faith for dying as she did for living.

There were many things to admire about Tracey's life. It would be hard to say any one thing had more impact than the others did. However, I most admired that Tracey was writing her own legacy out of the love she had for her little boy. Even after reconciling herself to the reality of death, she was still determined to live out the rest of her life as a strong witness for Jesus and an example for Joey.

Chapter 22

Joey's Greatest Gift

Over the years, I recorded various music projects that included many of the songs I had written. Tracey, however, never wanted to record an album. She always felt her voice was not good enough to rationalize the cost of doing one. In addition, she didn't feel as though she traveled enough to properly promote one. She thought people wanted to see and hear a person before they purchased their album. Therefore, I never pushed her to do one until after our talk about dying.

When I first approached Tracey with the idea, she was very opposed to it. She had a list of reasons why she should not do an album. She said, "Why should I do an album if I'm not going to be alive to perform it. I don't think we should be spending money for an album right now. We're going to need all the money we can get if I really get sick. Anyways, I'm not interested in doing a memorial album. I think the whole idea is morbid. It's cruel of you to ask me to do this right now. I'm fighting for my life and all you can think of is me doing an album?"

Okay! This was going to be easy. NOT! Instead of denying anything Tracey said, I admitted she was right except for the part about being morbid and cruel. I explained to her that I felt God had given her a beautiful voice, but even a more wonderful testimony.

My first idea was to do a videotape of her sharing a message for Joey. The more I thought about it, I realized what she would say to Joey, others needed to hear as well. For years, she had communicated so well through the avenue of music so why stop now.

I wanted her to do an album of songs but also share her testimony. I assured her I was not attempting to exploit her life, but rather share it. I challenged her to think of it as keeping her message alive and not herself. As for the cost, it was the least of my concern.

Tracey eventually agreed to do the project, doing it more for me than for herself. She was willing to yield when I felt strongly about doing something especially if I made a good case for it being right.

I contacted my friend Hal Wright who had done numerous projects for me in the past. He was a genius when it came to writing and producing music, a master at getting the most for your money. We also asked our good friend Stephanie to sing background on a couple of Tracey's favorite songs. It meant so much to both of us.

We decided to record nine songs in all and then have Tracey share her testimony at the very end. I picked out most of the songs while she concentrated more on writing her testimony. Some were songs Tracey loved to sing while others focused on more of the message she wanted to share.

She had the final word obviously, but didn't change anything I chose. Similarly, I didn't suggest any changes to the testimony she had written. As usual, it was a team effort. We called it *"Tracey...A Testimony."*

It was difficult for Tracey to work in the studio. By this time, the pain in her hip was getting worse and worse, making it hard for her to find any position to sit in where it would be comfortable. Tracey didn't like the way her medicine made her feel so she would only take it when the pain became unbearable. Nevertheless, she was able to fight through it and do a wonderful job. Many singers try to mimic the sound of pain in their songs. Unfortunately, Tracey's was real.

After Tracey completed her album, we asked Pastor Charlie if we could debut it at the church, he consented and a date was set. In the meantime, I thought about the concert and ways we could make it special.

Our house was always full of music and everyone participated. Joey had a very nice voice for his age and loved to sing with his mommy. I came up with the idea of having Joey sing a duet with Tracey, what a great gift that would be. It would be even better if it were a surprise.

I sat down with Joey and shared my thoughts with him. He was only seven but I felt he was old enough to do it. He just sat there motionless and offered no comment. He didn't have to say a word, his answer was written all over his face. I asked him again only this time I demanded a response. While shaking his head sideways he replied, "I don't want to."

I asked, "Why not?"

He came back with my least favorite answer and one he knew was never acceptable, "I don't know." I suggested he did know why and I needed to know before I would stop asking.

Joey started to cry and said, "Daddy, I just don't want to."

I picked Joey up and snuggled him, telling him I would never make him sing so he could quit crying. I asked him to listen to what I had to say.

"Joey, I know you don't feel like you want to do this. It's all right not to want to. I just don't want you to grow up and look back wishing you had done it. It's okay to be scared; it's okay to feel uncomfortable.

"I'm not asking you to do this because you want to. I'm asking you to do it for mommy. If you think about yourself, it will be hard, if you think about doing it for mommy, it will be easier. Sometimes it's okay to feel uncomfortable if it means making someone else happy.

"Son, a great man does what he doesn't want to do when he doesn't want to do it. No one can make you want to do this other than yourself. Will you at least think about it and tell me your answer tomorrow? Maybe you can pray about it tonight and ask Jesus what you should do. Whatever you decide will be fine. I won't bring it up again."

Joey agreed to think about it. As he was walking away he said, "I already know that I'm not gonna want to tomorrow either." He turned around to catch my response but I pretended not to hear him.

Yes, I wanted Joey to do this as a gift for Tracey, but I wanted it even more for him. I couldn't tell him he needed to sing with his mommy because she was going to die. However, I knew he was old enough to remember our conversation one day. I didn't want Joey to look back with any regrets after his mommy was gone for I knew living with regret could be very painful. I was just trying to save him from as much hurt as possible, *the future already held enough*. The final decision still had to be his.

The next day Joey came to me and said with excitement, "I decided to sing with mommy."

I asked surprisingly, "You are, why?"

Joey confidently replied, "Because I want to make mommy happy."

My heart was truly blessed but I still wanted to make sure he didn't feel pressured.

"Are you sure you're doing this because you want to or because daddy wants you to?"

Joey assured me he was doing it because he wanted to. My little boy had grown into a young man overnight. Not only will he make his mommy happy, but he will also make Jesus happy. I could only hope he would always want to make Jesus happy.

Joey's favorite song to sing on Tracey's album was the Gaither tune, *Because He Lives*. He and I practiced the song for hours until he had it down pat. I would even have Joey sing it with Tracey around the house. She had no clue what was going on. It was our fun secret, although mommy sometimes wondered why we were always whispering and laughing behind her back. We needed to be careful so we didn't let the "cat out of the bag."

Joey seemed fine the day of the concert so I didn't have to worry about him backing out. He had the courage to see the whole thing through to the end. Tracey sang most of the songs on her album while sharing a little of what each one meant to her. When it came time for Tracey to sing *Because He Lives* I interrupted her by talking over her. She had no idea what was going on so she got a little ticked at me for doing so.

I announced that Tracey was going to sing a duet and it was going to be with Joey. Tracey looked at me with raised eyebrows as if to ask, "Okay, what are you up to now, Denny?" I was always in trouble so what else was new.

It took her a moment for everything to sink in as Joey joined her on stage. She immediately began to make him feel as comfortable as possible. When she was sure he was ready, I started the music.

Joey stood beside his mommy's wheelchair with his eyes locked into hers, never once looking at the congregation. After all, he wasn't doing this for them, only his mommy. Tracey followed suit and the two of them sang to each other as if no one else was even there. In his nervousness, Joey's little hips kept rocking back and forth in time with the music.

He was so cute that everyone was laughing and crying both at the same time. Tracey was encouraging Joey throughout the entire song with a constant nodding of her head.

Both of them hit the big note at the end of the song with everything they had. You could see every vein in Joey's neck as he strained to hold the note as long as his mommy did. Tracey's voice faltered as she began to cry, "You did so good. You did so good."

Singing with Joey was overwhelming for Tracey. So many emotions had to be flowing inside her heart and mind, it would be futile to try to imagine or attempt to describe what she was feeling at that moment. Those emotions were personal, known only by Tracey, meant only for Joey.

Tracey loved all the things Joey made for her in school. Some of them were silly and some of them were nice. Some of them were artistic while others were so bad we didn't have the nerve to ask what they were. As long as the present was from her "Jahji," the nickname Tracey gave to Joey, it was perfect.

However, none of those gifts compared to the one Joey gave his mommy the day he decided to sing with her. Tracey knew how hard it was for him to sing in front of so many people. By doing so, he was proving just how much he really loved her. *His love was her greatest gift.*

Watching the two of them sing together was also a special gift to me. However, Tracey's gift to Joey was just as significant or more so. The duet put the two of them face to face with each other. This gave Tracey the opportunity to look straight into Joey's eyes and sing the words that would have been so hard to say otherwise. *"And then one day, I'll cross that river. I'll fight life's final war with pain. And then as death, gives way to victory. I'll see the lights of glory and I'll know He reigns."*

Somehow, I believe those words were planted into Joey's heart for a reason that day. Those words were not just another verse to a song; *it was the last verse of Tracey's life.* Knowing and believing them would prepare Joey's heart for when his mommy went to heaven.

Joey understood that his mommy knew Jesus as her personal savior. He knew that because Jesus lives, his mommy will live, only now with Jesus in heaven. He will miss his mommy, but not her hurting. She won't have to hurt or cry anymore, she won't need any more medicine or operations. Mommy will be able to feel good all the time. She will be happy living with Jesus, so we can be happy for her even if she's gone.

Most children will mirror how their parents act or feel and because of that, I didn't worry about Joey. When it came time for him to face his mommy's death, he would respond in the same way she did, with faith and courage. Is it too much to ask? *I guess it depends on the example.*

Chapter 23

Broken Again

Tracey's cancer was starting to get worse, she was not responding to the chemotherapy or radiation treatments in the way we had hoped. There was no relief from the pain and her use of medication needed to be increased. At that point, the doctors had already confirmed that continuing with treatment was pointless. Nevertheless, as long as Tracey wanted to go on, they would continue.

I'll never forget the last time we went to see Dr. Rehmus. The two of them talked about future chemotherapy treatments. She was upfront with Tracey when she let her know the hope of having any success with the chemo was slim to none. She would continue to prescribe treatment but suggested Tracey might consider not getting sick any longer and enjoy some quality time. Tracey could think about it and let her know her decision later.

Before we left, the doctor asked me to sit in the waiting room while she talked with Tracey, alone. I never knew the content of their conversation but I do know Esther gave Tracey something much stronger than chemo, compassion. It wasn't a doctor/ patient talk; no, they just had a good old "girl to girl cry". God knew Tracey would need this woman doctor at the end, not for what a wonderful doctor she could be, but for what a compassionate person she was.

During this time, I had to keep myself in good physical condition so I could help Tracey, even with the simplest of things. I was now picking Tracey up and moving her around much more than before, it was the only way to keep weight off her hip. I wanted to protect her from any more pain or injury. When I lifted her, I always needed to position myself in a way that was right for her but bad for me. My back was especially subject to precarious positions so I began lifting weights three times a week.

Tracey needed my help most with going to the bathroom. We were at a point where privacy was not an option. It was easier to carry Tracey than for her to try to maneuver her wheelchair through a maze of furniture. In addition, the doorway into the bathroom wasn't wide enough for the wheelchair to fit through.

I would first stand her up, then with my cheek next to hers and my arms around her waist lift as gently as possible. I would arch my back so some of her weight would rest on my chest. I did this to keep from squeezing her too tight. Tracey would hold on by placing both her arms around my neck as tightly as she could as I slowly carried her into the bathroom.

I would hold her with one arm while disrobing her with the other. I would ease her onto the seat as lightly as possible so she would not get hurt. About this time, we were closer than two people would ever want to be.

One night while sitting her down, I heard a popping sound and felt something snap in her back. Tracey's face grimaced slightly but that wasn't unusual, most movements caused her pain. I checked to see if she was all right and she thought so except for some discomfort in her back.

From then on Tracey started having more and more pain in her back. It finally got to the point where I couldn't move her at all without it hurting her so I had the paramedics transport her to the hospital. The x-rays revealed that Tracey had a broken back from another tumor that was growing in her spine.

I felt so bad. I blamed myself for breaking her back. It made me sick to my stomach to think her back broke right when I was holding her. I was trying so hard to keep her from hurting but now I was the one causing the harm. The doctor told me her back would have broken regardless and that I shouldn't blame myself. The only thing I was guilty of was trying to take good care of Tracey.

While in the hospital, more tests uncovered that Tracey's shoulder was also broken. The cancer was now growing more rampant than ever before. Even some small tumors on her clavicle were visible to the naked eye.

I met with the surgeons to find out what recourse we had, if any. It was the consensus that pain management should be our most urgent option. They decided to do surgery on Tracey's back and shoulder but only to help reduce the pain. The procedure was just to cement the broken areas, not to do any reconstruction. The only way to help Tracey at this point was to try to keep her out of pain.

One night during visiting hours, Tracey was so heavily drugged she couldn't have an intelligible conversation so I went home. Joey was staying all night with my parents that night so it was just the dog and me.

The longer I sat, the more depressed I got. Up until then there was always a plan to follow or something to focus on. I was a control freak who was living in an "out of control" situation and feeling helpless. I knew God was there and although I felt his presence, I didn't want to be comforted, at least right then. I was angry and wanted to stay that way for a while. I never wanted to talk to God when I was angry, especially if I wasn't willing to stop. I knew I wasn't ready to let go of the anger, so I was avoiding him for the time being.

I knew God was in control of our situation but it was still so hard to accept. There was a big difference between living knowing Tracey was going to die, and living watching her die. *The latter did not resemble living to me.*

I felt more alone than ever. Even our dog Chelsea recognized my anger and stayed away from me. I was my own worst enemy but the only one I was talking with. The anger I was feeling took me back to the days when I handled everything with booze. I got in my car and drove around for over an hour. I went through a drive-thru two different times to buy some beer, only to order a soft drink. Part of me, the hurting one, wanted to escape even for just one night, the other part, the rational one, knew it was wrong. Unfortunately, I listened to the hurting me instead, buying the beer the third time through.

I went to an out of town drive-thru so no one would recognize me. I didn't want to blow my witness as I was preparing to get drunk. How's that for hypocrisy? The fellow at the drive-thru turned out to be an unlikely "Good Samaritan."

"What do you need buddy?"

"I need something to take me away for a night."

"What did you say?"

"Oh, never mind, a six pack of Stroh's."

There I was sitting in the middle of a drive-thru explaining that my wife was dying of cancer to someone who probably didn't even care. I told him I hadn't had a drink in fourteen years but I needed to escape reality, even for just a moment. After listening to me ramble, the fellow went to the cooler bringing back another six-pack.

"Here buddy, this one's on me. I think you're going to need it."

I appreciated the young man's compassion. In his own way, he was offering a cup of cold water to a needy man only in the form of a cold beer. The similarity just might be the same.

I'm sure most Christians will find this part of my book disturbing; it was disturbing to write. How could a preacher allow himself to get so low that he could buy beer instead of pray? *I guess you had to be there.*

I went back to the house and sat, staring at the beer. I was still wrestling with myself, but eventually the wrong fellow won. I opened three bottles and chugged all of them straight down. I did this when I was younger; it helped me get drunk a lot faster. I then proceeded to drink the rest of the twelve beers. Although I didn't escape, the pain was numbed for a short while.

Later, I remembered that I was supposed to be the "special music" in church the next morning so I called Pastor Charlie. I told him I was drinking and didn't think it was right for me to sing in church. Even while drunk I still felt accountable. I didn't want to be a bad example to anyone else.

Charlie was disappointed in me and rightfully so. I just wanted him to understand how much I was hurting. I needed a friend that night, not a sermon. I'm sure I would give myself one in the morning. Charlie offered to come to my house and talk with me but I told him it might not be safe for him. I was always a mean drunk so I was just trying to protect the friend I loved.

I woke up the next morning remembering why I stopped drinking years before. I felt lousy, deservingly so. Our situation was the still the same, nothing had changed except now I had a horrible hangover. Drinking didn't make anything better, only worse. Drugs and alcohol never solve any problem; they only disguise it. I put my life and all my problems back into God's hands, throwing away the mask.

Christmas came and went during this stay in the hospital and it was the saddest one we ever experienced. One of the main themes of Christmas is hope, but there was none for us that year. I don't remember enough to write about; I spent too much time trying to forget it. We did our best to at least make it fun for Joey although I'm not sure how successful we were.

Tracey and I talked previously about what to do when her condition worsened. She asked me to promise I wouldn't put her in any kind of care facility. Her wish was to die in her own home where she could spend her last days close to her family. To this point, I tried to be faithful to all her requests. This was not an exception; home it would be.

Tracey made me promise I would not allow Joey to stay around her if things got too bad. She didn't want him to be scared or have horrible memories of her. She trusted me to make that decision when it was time.

I prepared a bedroom for Tracey in the far end of the home but that didn't last for very long. She felt out of touch with everyone so we moved her bed into the living room. There she was able to be right in the thick of things.

Tracey was now in "survival mode." Her body was using most of its energy trying to fight off the cancer causing her to sleep most of time. The morphine she was taking only helped to accentuate the situation. Her level of patience was slowly fading as well. Joey received most of her patience, her mom got a little, and I got none. I would not have had it any other way.

Tracey's mom spent as much time at the house as possible. She helped me with so much over the years I could have never gotten through it without her. We didn't spend alot of time appreciating each other, we just did. We both realized Tracey and Joey needed the attention, so we did for them. That itself was a way for us to thank each other.

My heart broke for Shirley whenever she looked at her precious daughter. Every tear she shed for Tracey carried a different emotion. There were tears filled with pride, others full of pain. Some carried memories of happy times and sad times, but mostly smiles. Several tears filled up with worry while more held on to hope. However, altogether they overflowed with love. I knew how losing my wife made me feel but I could never imagine what Shirley must have felt to be losing her child. God gave Shirley a special grace.

I grew more depressed as Tracey grew worse. I could not even grieve for I was all grieved out. Until then there was always the fight or the next step to look forward to, even if it were something negative. There was always some way for me to help Tracey, but now it seemed as though I served no purpose and could no longer make a difference. I lost my wife the same day I lost my hope. Everyone told me I was a good caregiver for Tracey but there was nothing left for me to do except watch her die. *I had no desire to be good at that.*

I started to feel sorry for myself and I was ashamed for doing so. How could I feel sorry for myself when Tracey was the one who was dying? But part of me was dying. My wife, who was part of me, was dying. Part of my family was dying. My son's mommy was dying. Our ministry together was dying. Our shared friendships were dying.

I needed help but was too embarrassed to ask for it. It wasn't because of pride; I just felt Tracey deserved all the attention. Anyways, too many eyes were watching to start showing weakness. I wanted everyone to see that God was big enough to carry me all the way.

Looking back, I realize God did not need defending. Both Tracey and I could have done a better job of helping others by allowing ourselves to be even more transparent with all our failings. God's strength reveals itself most when a person exposes his or her weakness. I learned that a weakness by itself leads to failure, while a weakness dependent upon God's strength will lead to victory. God is not calling all of us to be superheroes, just obedient servants.

Up to this point, I felt I had done well for Tracey. *I just didn't want to fail the final exam.*

Chapter 24

Time to Go Home

The doctors originally thought Tracey might live another six months after going home but it was only speculative. There was no real way of telling how fast the cancer would spread and where. After about a month, it seemed Tracey's time to live was going to be even shorter. The hospice representatives that frequently visited reported that Tracey's heart rate was getting faster and faster with each visit. This was another indication that time was running out.

It was now the beginning of February in 1993. Shirley called her daughter Lori who lived near San Francisco. She made her aware of Tracey's condition while letting her know that it was time to come home to be with her sister. She made prompt arrangements to come back to Ohio to visit Tracey, knowing it was probably for the last time. Before Lori came, Tracey had been very lethargic and out of it for most of the time. We were keeping her heavily sedated to help with the pain so I was starting to wish Lori had come sooner.

God blessed us with so many memories over the years, but he was not through yet. It was as if he was saying, "One more time." He had a special gift for Lori and Tracey as well as Shirley.

After Lori arrived, there was a short period of time when Tracey's pain subsided; enough that she didn't need as much medicine. Because of that, she was very alert and able to be herself. This seemed to be God's way of allowing Lori to have some quality time with her big sister. They spent many afternoons just talking and laughing together, reminiscing about the past while trying to avoid talking about the future.

Lori helped Tracey work on a scrapbook she was making for Joey containing pictures and memories that would help Joey remember the wonderful times they had together. Tracey had already spent countless hours putting it together, but now felt the urgency to complete it. It was a true labor of love.

One day, Tracey had Lori go into Joey's bedroom to get a puppet she named *Smarty Pants*. Tracey was the smart-alecky voice that brought the little stinker to life. She began to entertain Lori just as they did when they were small. Tracey was so funny they all laughed until they cried. The fun lasted for only a short moment however the memory it created will last for a lifetime.

Many family members as well as friends also visited Tracey. It was a special memory for them as well as very sad. One of the most important visits Tracey had was with her dad. She knew it was time to confront him about their relationship even though most of her life she felt uncomfortable talking with him, especially about relationships. Until then, she just let him say or do whatever he wanted but now time was running out. If she was ever going to say what was on her heart, it needed to be then.

Tracey told her dad how much she loved him and that all she ever wanted from him was to know he loved her. It was hard for Tracey to say but I'm sure even harder for him to hear. There was a tender heart inside that tough exterior just breaking for his daughter. Chuch assured Tracey he loved her and always had. He told her how proud he was of her and what a wonderful daughter she was, apologizing for not being closer with her. Reconciling with her father was more than just something Tracey wanted, it was something she always needed, and so did he.

Tracey's good days were short lived. I noticed she was starting to act incoherent around Joey and I could see it was disturbing to him. She was beginning to fail even more causing Joey to feel uncomfortable seeing his mommy in that condition. One day, Joey asked me why his mommy was acting the way she was. I knew then it was time for me to do something. I was torn between whom I needed to protect more, Joey or Tracey. I remembered promising Tracey I would not let Joey watch her suffer which made my decision easier, but not without pain. I decided to take him to my parent's house to stay, knowing he would get lots of love and care from them.

Joey didn't realize when he hugged and kissed his mommy goodbye it would be for the last time, however everyone else did. Tracey was still somehow able to protect Joey by not making his departure traumatic. I don't know how conscious she was of what was happening, but it made it easier for Joey. It was much harder for Shirley as she struggled so hard to control her feelings. I could almost hear her heart breaking as she watched Tracey say goodbye to her little boy. Lori was hurting for both Tracey and her mom as her own heart took a beating.

On the way to my parent's house, Joey asked why he had to leave. I told him mommy was feeling really bad and didn't want him to see her so sick. He looked at me and said, "I know dad, she's been sick for a long time." I wondered just how much Joey actually realized.

Tracey's body was starting to shut down. On her last visit, the woman from hospice told me she didn't expect

Tracey to last very long. Our prayers for healing surrendered to prayers for mercy, those who had once prayed for Tracey's life to be spared were now praying it would peacefully end. Everyone was willing to let go of Tracey if it meant letting go of her suffering.

On February 17, the three of us were sitting around the dining room table when a sound coming from the living room interrupted our conversation. As we entered the room, I recognized what the hospice worker had described as the "death rattle." Tracey was dying, breathing her last breaths before leaving to see Jesus.

We surrounded her bed, quietly waiting for her to pass. There were no signs of struggle or suffering only a sense of peace. Any sadness turned to celebration as we envisioned the angels ushering Tracey into *Glory*. It was an honor and privilege to attend her eternal homecoming. *Surely, the presence of the Lord was in that place.*

After the funeral home came for Tracey, everyone left. It was time for me to get my little boy. I called my parents and told them Tracey had passed but to please not let Joey know. I wanted to tell him myself, alone.

When we got back to the house, I took Joey into the living room. I sat him on my lap with his legs straddling mine. This way I could look straight into his face. I had a hard time opening my mouth to say anything so Joey broke the silence by asking, "Where's mommy?" I wanted so much to keep my composure, but I couldn't. As I looked into his precious little face, I began to cry while saying, "Mommy died Joey. She went to heaven to be with Jesus." I began to cry even harder. As I did, Joey started stroking my face, wiping the tears away. Without shedding even a tear he sort of smiled as he said, "Daddy, it's all right. Now mommy doesn't have to hurt no more. Now she can be happy."

Instead of me comforting Joey, he was comforting me. He was able to stand courageous even in this saddest time because of the example Tracey had been to him for all his life. He accepted her death in the way she accepted her own. He was part of her, and she will always be part of him.

No one really knows what Heaven is like exactly. The Bible gives us some idea but lets us know it is more than what we could ever imagine. God made man in his own image therefore I believe there might be some similarities between our earthly bodies and the ones we get in heaven. With that said, this is what I pictured happening right after Tracey arrived in Heaven.

Tracey hit the "streets of gold" running as fast as she could. Along the way, many friends and family who had gone on before her were anxiously calling out to her, "Tracey, stop, the reunion has just begun."

Tracey kept running only to respond, "I'll be right back, I've got to find Jesus."

When she came to a huge crowd singing and praising God, she knew she was close to Jesus.

She thought to herself, "How am I ever going to get close enough to thank Jesus for saving me?"

Just then, a voice called out for everyone to step aside. "Let my child come to me for I've been waiting for her."

Tracey walked through the crowd and kneeled at Jesus' feet. He said, "Well done, my good and faithful servant. Well done."

As Tracey stood up, she realized for the first time she had both her legs. She was so excited to see Jesus she never noticed. She started to thank him, but could only stare at the holes in his feet and hands. Although Tracey was now perfect, she realized that Jesus still bore the scars of Calvary. *They remain as an eternal reminder of the sacrifice he made so she might have everlasting life.*

Epilogue

*H*undreds of people attended the memorial service held for Tracey. Notice I referred to it as a memorial service and not a funeral. We were there to celebrate Tracey's life, not mourn her death. In fact, when the doctor pronounced her dead, Tracey was never *more alive* than at that moment. The Bible teaches *"to be absent from the body is to be present with the Lord."* Tracey was not only alive, but also completely healed, never to hurt, or cry, or feel sorrow ever again.

One of her favorite songs to sing was *Home Where I Belong*. That song was never more real to her than the day she awoke and found herself face to face with her savior, Jesus. Instead of dreaming about heaven, she was living it. She was only *passin' through* during her short time here on earth. She finally made it home where all the yesterdays, todays, and tomorrows add up to be what is called eternity. Tracey is "home where she belongs."

Tracey's faith turned her tragedies into triumphs, her failures into opportunities, and her fears into hope.

In many ways, Tracey's handicap was more of a blessing than it was a bad thing. It forced her to slow down, allowing her to experience the little things so many of us miss as we race through life. Cancer didn't rob her of her life; it just helped to define what her life was going to be and what a difference it would make to others.

Tracey knew her life would be short so she made each day longer by living it to the fullest. It's not what was taken away from Tracey that will be most remembered, but what she gave back; not what she lost, but how much she gained.

I'm not sure how accurate it is to even say that Tracey's life was cut short. Whose standards should we use to measure how long a person should live, God's, or ours? Our opinion would carry a personal bias because of how it affects us. Selfishly, when we love someone, we want him or her to live forever or at least longer than us. We don't want to experience the loss or loneliness that accompanies death, therefore the thought of separation can even blind us to his or her pain and suffering.

God's purpose for someone expands far greater than what we have the ability to see or understand, especially in the midst of trials and difficulty. Because of his omniscience, God sees the victory even before the war is declared. Although God's design is for us to enjoy and love one another, he created us mainly for his own purpose. That purpose is for us to know him, live for him, and tell others about him.

The purpose of this book is to tell others about him, to show not only how Jesus blessed our family when Tracey was alive, but also how he continues to bless far beyond anything imaginable.

In the summer of Tracey's death, I preached at a family camp in Michigan. On one of the nights, I preached a strong message on sin and its consequence. Joey sat in the front row with a coloring book where I could keep an eye on him. He was very quiet, glancing up only occasionally. At the end of the message, Joey came forward and asked Jesus to forgive him for his sins. What a privilege it was to have my own son accept Christ under my preaching.

From that moment, Joey has continued to walk with the Lord. God has blessed him with not only a loving heart but also a wonderful mind. Joey graduated from high school in 2003 with a 3.92 GPA. He is now a junior at Miami University in Oxford, Ohio where he's double majoring in finance and economics. I'm not sure where God will lead Joey, but I'm definite he will never walk alone. God has truly answered Tracey's prayers for her little boy.

I became good friends with a beautiful lady in my church named Wendy. She had an infectious personality and energy measurable only by a "Richter scale." Wendy was a "health nut" and "fitness freak," the very essence of a healthy lifestyle. I must admit I was attracted to her because of it, but mostly because she loved the Lord.

Wendy was there for me when I was at my lowest, challenging me to pick myself up and live life to the fullest. When push came to shove, she used a *bulldozer*.

This made me think of Tracey's words. "Just because my life is going to end doesn't mean yours has to." I decided to live.

I believed God chose Wendy not only to be my wife, but also to be a mom for Joey. Marrying her has brought love and healing to our home as well as a lot of joy. She's been a great mom to Joey, loving him as if he were her own. This was just another of Tracey's many answered prayers.

Wendy and I also have a son together. We named him Caleb Joseph; Caleb, because the Caleb of the Bible followed the Lord with his whole heart; and Joseph, after his big brother. Caleb has his mommy's energy and his daddy's desire to preach. At eleven years old, he already has a burden for all of his friends to know Jesus.

Caleb and Joey love each other very much. Their relationship is special, refusing to consider themselves as stepbrothers. They're both my boys, my seed that makes them brothers.

Our whole family has continued to have a close relationship with Tracey's mom, Shirley. In no way did losing Tracey cause us to lose our love for one another; it has only grown.

Shirley still considers me her son-in-law. We went through a lot together, sharing the same heartbreaks and joys through loving the same person, even in different ways. We'll always have a special bond.

Joey has also continued to stay very close with his *Grandma Bob*, the name he gave Shirley when he first started to talk. Shirley kept her promise to Tracey by telling Joey all the little things about her that she would never get the chance to share. Something only a "mommy of a mommy" could do best.

Caleb also has a unique relationship with *Shirley Bob*, another name our family has given her. When Caleb was very young, he found it hard to understand why Shirley was Joey's grandma and not his. Therefore, Shirley promptly adopted him as her grandchild, treating him no different from Joey.

I'm sure Joey and Caleb sit at the top of Shirley's prayer list. There's nothing like having a "praying grandma" in your corner while growing up.

Shirley and Wendy have become unbelievably close. Their friendship started from a common interest and love for Joey, but grew into a mutual admiration and love for one another, a tribute to God's healing and enabling grace.

You can find the two of them in church every Sunday sitting right beside each other. Theirs is a story in itself waiting to be written.

Shirley is a special person deserving "extra special" love.

God is so good!

If you found this story to be sad you might consider reading it again, only this time look closer at all the wonderful things God did for our family. He never left us, he never forgot us and he was there all the time.

Many people might find themselves asking why God allowed all of this to happen, especially to a good Christian woman. To help you try to understand you must first try to understand God.

I'll agree that it is impossible for anyone to totally comprehend everything about God; our minds don't have the capacity, that's why faith is so important. However, we *can* learn a lot about the nature of God and the way he thinks through reading the Bible and knowing him personally as a born again believer. It's hard to give credence to anyone who claims to know who God is or what he thinks if their opinion doesn't align with his Word, the Holy Bible.

The Bible says, *"...He (God) causes his sun to rise on the evil and the good, and sends rain on the righteous and the unrighteous."* (Matthew 5:45) Here, Jesus is saying that no one (good or bad) is exempt from "problems and trials" or "pain and suffering."

We may never know *why* bad things happen, however we can know *who* to go to *when* they do happen, Jesus. *"...we are more than conquerors through him who loved us. For I am convinced that neither death nor life, neither angels nor demons, neither the present nor the future, nor any powers, neither height nor depth, nor anything else in all creation, (Not even cancer) will be able to separate us from the love of God that is in Christ Jesus our Lord."* (Romans 8:37-39)

Being a Christian does not always mean you will have a great life, it means you will be great *for* life.

Through my story, I hope you have seen Jesus. I hope you have heard him. I invite you to know him, so you can be great *for* life.

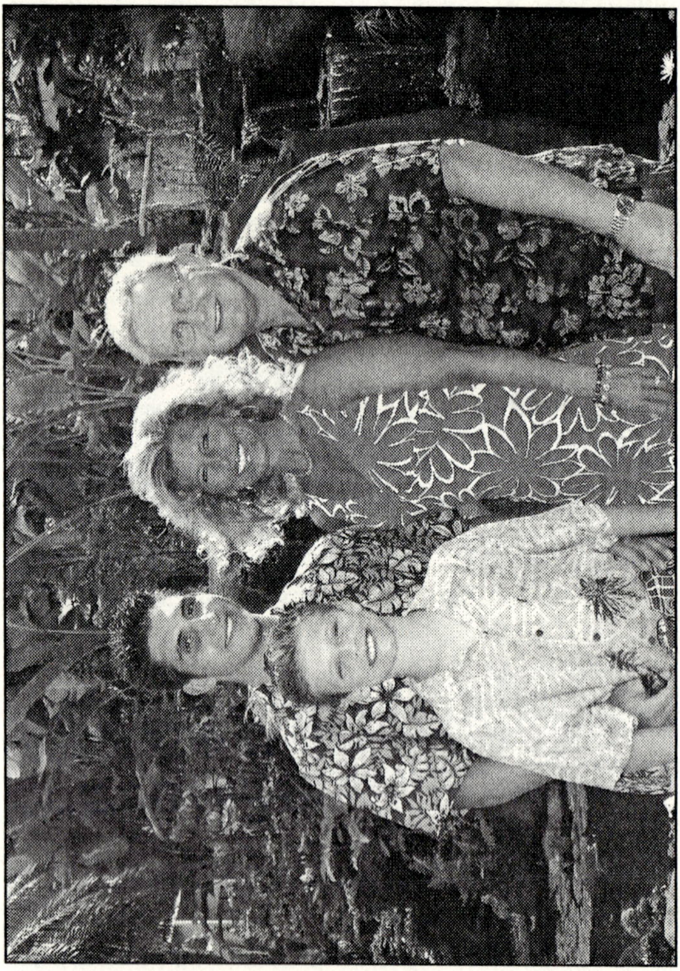

Contact

To contact Denny Kleibscheidel for speaking engagements and or concerts go to www.dennyk.org.